GANGA REVIEW

2023

Ganga Review ISSN 1930-0662 is published annually in the United States by Chintamani Books. The journal is a member of the Community of Literary Magazines and Presses. Issues are printed in accordance with the Sustainable Forestry Initiative. For every magazine purchased, a tree is planted.

Submission Guidelines: Please submit up to five poems or one work of prose per envelope. Include SASE and contact information (name, address, telephone, email). Work should be previously unpublished. We accept first North American serial rights. Kindly post to Submittable.

Address correspondence to:

Ganga Review
110 West 86th St., Suite 5D
New York, NY 10024

Subscriptions are $12 for one year, plus $5.50 postage and handling.

Lalitamba Foundation is a 501(c)3 nonprofit organization. Proceeds from magazine sales are used for charitable purposes, including prison book distribution and shelter for vulnerable women. The journal is also donated to hospitals, shelters, and other communities in need throughout the United States. Further contributions are tax-deductible according to New York State law.

Website: www.lalitamba.com
Facebook: https://www.facebook.com/Lalitamba-252686692751/

ISBN 978-1-7324541-9-4

The journal was inspired by a bhajan sung on a pilgrimage through India. In early 2004, we traveled through the country with India's "hugging saint" to alleviate the suffering that comes with poverty, illness, and plain loss of hope. The journal was founded when we returned to New York City in November of that year.

The journal is named for the sacred River Ganga.

TABLE OF CONTENTS

LETTERS AND PRAYERS

He wrote a word on a sheet of paper,
a word that shook and trembled and spoke.
He looked at it and didn't know
how or why or where it came from.
He read it and reread it,
though it was but one word,
yet it filled him with light
and bliss and joy.
He sat on the grass under a tree,
the notepad in his hand,
but no other word
would come from his pen;
yet his eyes shone like a light,
and there was something like a halo over his head.
I looked over his shoulder,
and the word on his pad
was God.

Jay Frankston
Little River, CA

If you say the word God
not use it, just say it
without attaching a definition,
without searching for a meaning—

If you say the word God
without a prayer or supplication at the end,
without a visual or imaginary being in your mind—

If you say the word God under your breath,
as a whisper or a scream of hopelessness and despair,
if you say it often enough, this word God,
so full of all there is, so rich in time and space,
so infinite and eternal—

If you say it often enough,
God God God
say it, count it 'til you stop counting,
not with conviction, not with faith or belief,
just the word God repeated
over and over again
for an uninterrupted period of time,
the word will not enter through your brain
and seek to define itself.
It will enter through your heart.

Just say the word God.
God God God
The feeling will penetrate your soul,
and the word will open up.

You will be filled with the light of the word,
and God will be with you for an instant.

Jay Frankston
Little River, CA

The journal is an offering for liberation.
May all beings be joyful and free.

Peter L. Scamardo

THE GIRL WHO LIVED IN AN AIRPORT

If I hadn't been reclined, I might not have noticed the little black leather wallet beneath my chair. I imagine whomever it belonged to had only just forgotten it and was now flying off on the Lufthansa flight I had been watching. The poor sucker.

I knelt down to pick the wallet up. What else was I supposed to do? If I didn't pick it up, then someone else would, and I was hungry. The face in the wallet was of someone named Robert Forester. Mr. Forester had left me eight dollars in his wallet. I didn't bother with the other bits of plastic.

I thought that eight dollars could go a long way, that it might be worth saving. I also thought that one of those cheese steaks in the food court would taste amazing. I hadn't had one in eight months. Just the thought of them made my stomach twist. So, I put the wallet back where I'd found it and headed in that direction.

Compared to the lifeless arrival and departure gates, the food court and shopping area were full of life. They had to be. All the bright lights, mouth-watering smells, and attractive scents had to give people hope, as they for waited hours to board their flights out of Pittsburgh.

I made sure to walk through the perfume shop on my way over. I loved the variety of fragrances I would find there on any given day. Plus, they helped hide my natural musky odor.

The fella at the cheese steak shop gave me what I wanted without any trouble. He was too exhausted by the droves of people he had served that day to think twice about the nine-year-old girl at the stand. Usually, the employees assumed I was the daughter of the person ordering behind me. This was an early taste of independence, I suppose. Little did they realize.

I liked to sit between the escalators, while I ate. This position gave me a full view of the airport lounge. On either side were hallways that led to the gates. The food court was to my left, the perfume shop to my right, and a whole bevy of Pittsburgh memorabilia stores front and center. Or at least they would have been visible were it not for the twenty-foot Christmas tree planted in the center of the room.

It was mid-April. The employees at PIT were not getting an early start on the holidays. They had never taken the thing down. Travelers from near and far would pass through and wonder if some practical joke were being played on them. Some would think they had lost track of the seasons. What I enjoyed best was watching the kids ride up the escalator and dash toward the numerous colorful ribboned boxes at the base of the tree. If their parents tried to pull them back, they would shout in protest; but those who managed to open one of these boxes would still scream at the fact it was empty.

The scene was oddly nostalgic. The only thing I hated was that the tree got in the way of the plane hanging from the ceiling. It was a green fighter plane with a propeller engine at the front and two levels of wings. I'd have flown in one, if I were given the option. Perhaps, they did still have a few in reserve.

I looked up at the plane. Whenever the tree swayed ever so slightly, its branches knocked the plane into a swinging motion. More often than not, the plane looked as if it were going to fall onto the helpless people below.

It never did. The plane was stuck in the air, and I was stuck on the ground.

I turned my attention back to my meal.

"You know fellas," I said to the two gentlemen on either side of me, "if you want a bite, you only have to ask. You don't have to stare at me."

They said nothing. They didn't like to talk.

"Suit yourself," I said.

To my left was Franco Harris, the greatest running back ever to play the game of football. At least, that's what the man with the belly and the beard had to say about him, between bites of his Sloppy Joe.

To my right was George Washington. No one ever told me who he was.

They were two stoics in their own right. I liked that, though. PIT was so loud and boisterous. It was nice to have quiet people for company, people who didn't make noise just for the sake of making noise.

The quiet was broken by a loud shriek coming from the bottom of the escalator. There, I saw a young boy collapsed into tears. He had fallen in fear of Rex, our fifteen-foot-tall protector, and all four hundred of his serrated teeth. This happened more often than you'd expect. Yes, Rex was tall, and he had a lot of teeth, but he was nothing but bones. I mean, you could see right through him. Yet, time and time again, a child would collapse in fear from the sight of him.

"He really doesn't learn does he," I inquired of my companions.

They made no comment.

"He's supposed to scare people who are actually dangerous. Not kids."

Again, they gave no reply.

"Well since you two aren't going to do anything—"

I tossed my trash into a nearby bin and flew down the escalator. In seconds, I was on the ground floor and kneeling in front of the boy, having squeezed in between his parents to reach him.

"Hey, hey."

That seemed to get his attention, even if it may have startled his parents. He was still crying, but he was looking at me.

"Look at me, look at me," I said, trying to sound comforting.

"You see that fella? That's Rex. He's one to keep an eye on this here airport, but you needn't be afraid of him. He's all bones and no meat. Just look at him."

The boy stifled his cries for a moment to peer past me and up at Rex. He shrank back behind me upon his first glance, but at my urging, he looked back and didn't cower.

"You see. He can't hurt you. He's here to scare off all the bad people. That's not you."

The boy wiped away his tears and sniffled.

"By the look of your parents, you have some place to be. Now, you've got to be brave and get past Rex. Can you be brave for them?"

The boy nodded his head.

"Okay," I said with a reassuring smile.

Taking the boy's hand, I helped him up and then handed him to his mother. I watched, as he made his way up the escalator, past Rex, and into the bowels of PIT. He glanced back at me one last time, before disappearing inside.

His parents offered no words of thanks. An ungrateful lot. I did hear them ask each other who the strange little girl was.

In a way, I was surprised that they had noticed me. People almost never notice you when you're four feet tall.

I stayed down at the bottom of the escalator. I made sure to chastise Rex for scaring the boy, reminding him that he was meant to scare only dangerous people.

Three more trains of passengers disembarked and vanished beyond the escalators. I lost track of time, and before long, the lights were being dimmed. This happened every night. The shopkeepers were sent home. Passengers who had rooms in the hotel, or were members of the clubs, retired to their beds. Those who didn't were allowed to sleep at their terminals. This was why the lights were dimmed.

I ran my hands over Rex's name plate.

"Tire-anto-sower-us Rex. Good night, my friend."

I walked to the space behind Rex and knelt down. I made sure no one was watching, before I pressed against the paneling. This forgotten room was growing smaller and smaller with each passing year. Still, it was home. Here was where I laid my head on the piles of Steelers sweatshirts and wrapped myself tight in a Penguins blanket. I needed them, because the nights could get quite cold.

As I pulled the blanket up to my chest, I opened a tin can and counted the money inside, just as I did every night. One hundred and twenty-five dollars. Was that enough?

"Fly Emirates. Hello Tomorrow." That's what the pamphlet said. I had carried it with me for as long as I could remember. That, my passport, and a boarding pass for a flight to Singapore. I ran my fingers over the lion and the unicorn on the front of the passport.

"United Kingdom of Great Britain and Northern Ireland."

I opened my passport and looked at the photo inside. I couldn't have been more than two years old. My hair was bright blonde, and I was missing three teeth. The passport was on me, so it must've been mine. I couldn't remember not having it.

"Rose Conner," I read from the page. "Gloucester, GBR."

That was me. That was my home. Whatever way I had been lost, that was where they were waiting for me. All I had to do was get onto a plane and fly home.

I NEVER UNDERSTOOD WHY people came to PIT. There was nothing outside of the airport, apart from a bunch of hills. Then again, the snow could be pretty in the winter.

I liked hanging around the international wing the best. It was my domain, my kingdom. Here, I could sit for hours and listen to all the people who came through. I enjoyed hearing the different voices and watching the faces. I'd heard the Canadians, English, Scottish, and Australians, but the non-English speakers were always the best. The French and the Spanish, among others, had broad hand gestures and expressions that made me smile.

Of course, the main reason I enjoyed the international wing was that I needed to fly international. Why would I hang around flights headed for Denver or Houston? I needed to get to Gloucester.

I kept running the numbers in my head. I would need a countless number of dropped wallets, if I wanted to buy a ticket. Another another idea hovered in my mind, however. It was a crazy idea, but it was an idea.

Probably a thousand times, I had watched people scan their boarding passes. If the green light popped up, it meant they were okay to board, but the person's face never showed up on the screen.

Something I had noticed was that the adults would hand their tickets individually to the stewardesses. Yet, if there were a family, the parent would hand the clerk several tickets at once. I wondered whether, if there were a large enough family, I could slip in alongside them.

That day, I happened to spot one.

Larger than most families I had seen, this lot was seven in total. Two parents and five children. The oldest was probably ten, the youngest maybe three. The parents would rub their foreheads every other minute and breathe heavy sighs, while their children tugged on their arms and chattered at a glass-shattering volume. Stressed would be a mild way to describe the parents at that moment.

There was just enough chaos that I thought I might slip into line alongside them. It helped that they were a white, blondish family, but it helped even more that they were going to London. I don't know how far London is from Gloucester, but it was the UK. All I had to do was get there. I would figure it all out, afterward.

I wanted to run off to Rex, to tell him what I was about to do and to say goodbye, but I didn't have the time. I took my chances.

Everyone else in line was too preoccupied with their phones to notice me. The children were too busy with themselves. The parents were too busy with the tickets. Just as I had come to PIT unnoticed, so too, would I leave it.

Then, the youngest child of the family turned around. A boy of three with a golden-haired bowl cut, he was one of few people out there over whom I stood tall. He looked me up and down and then just stared. For three seconds, he stared at me, as if he knew I shouldn't have been there but didn't know what to do. Finally, he opened his mouth and uttered an ear-piercing screech that caused everyone in the area to turn in my direction.

It was as if, all this time, I had been in possession of a blanket that made me invisible, and now that blanket had just been ripped off of me. All of the children, the parents, and the people in line had turned to see a helpless little boy screaming in terror at a strange girl with greasy hair.

I was paralyzed. In the four years I had been at PIT, I had never once hesitated. Not once had I been afraid. Now, I was. I was uncertain what was going to happen next.

Out of the corner of my eye, I saw a security guard bearing down on me. As he came toward me, my blood got flowing and my feet were moving, once again.

I turned around and started walking away. Not running. Running would be bad. People who ran in airports got tackled to the ground. I walked. A little faster than a normal pace but still walking, regardless.

Glancing over my shoulder, I saw that the security guard was talking to the father of the family, who then pointed in my direction. We made eye contact, the security guard and I.

I groaned, as I realized the stupidity of the act. I couldn't just walk away now. I had to hide. Had to hide. For all I knew, the security guard was telling the others to be on the lookout for me. I couldn't run back to the storage room behind the panel. I might not even have time. I had to act fast.

With a quick a glance, I spotted a woman sitting by herself. Dirty blonde, wearing a red dress and a cardigan. I'm not sure why that resonated with me, but I acknowledged it. She seemed oblivious to what was going on around her, and there happened to be an open seat next to her.

I took the seat without saying anything and leaned as close as possible to her, so that it looked like we were sitting together. I was careful not to make her uncomfortable.

The woman had no reaction. She was completely engrossed in whatever magazine she was reading. I dared not look to see what that magazine was, so as to avoid her noticing me.

Still, I had not been seated for even a minute, before the security guard appeared in front of me. He didn't immediately grab me, as he might have had I been wandering the hall. He was staring down at me with a condescending look, but his main focus was on the woman next to me.

"Ma'am," he said.

She looked up at the man and put down her magazine. She still had not noticed me, so I leaned a little bit closer.

"May I have a word with your daughter?" he asked.

Naturally, the woman's perfectly smooth face stretched and scrunched to an expression of both shock and confusion. I did not give the woman a chance to tell the man that she didn't have a daughter, or if she did that it wasn't me. I grabbed hold of her left hand the moment the guard asked his question.

I took hold of her hand and slid low in the chair, looking my best to appear as a frightened little girl. I was afraid. Not of the guard, but of what he might make me do.

The moment that the woman spent gazing down at me felt like it would never end. The longer it lasted, the further I was falling into an inescapable black void.

Yet the woman never let go of my hand.

"What uh . . . what seems to be the problem?" the woman asked, turning her attention back to the guard.

It seemed I was safe for the moment. I looked up at the guard. Even he seemed surprised that the woman was coming to my defense. I tried to show no reaction, lest I expose myself.

"I have a concerned parent claiming your daughter scared his son," the guard said.

"Is this true?" the woman asked in what I assumed was the tone a mother used to speak to her child.

I froze for a moment, as I made eye contact with her. Looking at her face to face, only then did I realize how much I resembled her. It was an extra ordinary stroke of luck.

"I was just standing around. I was. The boy started screaming."

"Do you think you may have spooked him?" the woman asked.

"Probably," I said, trying to appear as innocent as possible. "But I don't know how, if I did . . . mama."

Every single hair on my head threatened to stand straight up, as I spoke. I could not explain how I came to say that word. I said it as if I had spit it out of my mouth a million times before. What was even more strange was that it felt like the right thing to say. In that moment, she was mama.

"Well, she's confessed officer," the woman said. "Is there anything else you would need her for?"

This, the guard had not expected. He had assumed, rightly so, that I was some unaccompanied minor who, in his eyes, was causing trouble. Without a doubt, he was set on throwing me into some detention cell. He was not expecting a parent to come to my aid. He couldn't punish a little girl who hadn't actually done anything.

"No ma'am," he finally said. "Take care."

This woman had come to my rescue. Although Franco and Rex had not moved an inch, this total stranger had helped me without any incentive. Now, I was safe once more.

We were still holding hands, even after the guard had gone. Neither one of us wanted to drop appearances, before it was totally safe.

I didn't want to let her go. Her presence was warm and comforting, but I had to be rational. I didn't know this woman. She was just as likely to whisk me away as the guard.

I had to leave, but when I started to walk away, I felt a tug on my right arm. She was still holding my hand.

"Now, wait a minute," she said.

I kicked her in the shins. I didn't think about it. I just did it.

Her grip loosened immediately, and I dashed off. By this point, the good people of PIT had resumed their regular activities. They were no longer distracted by the screaming of a child, nor was their gaze fixated on a greasy-haired little girl. Now, I was just another person. Invisible. No one notices you when you're four feet tall.

I zipped between the rows and rows of traveling people. I was lucky to have been running during the busiest time of day. So many people were crowded into PIT that I was little more than a phantom. Still, I did glance over my shoulder from time to time, to see if I was being followed. Once I reached Franco and saw that I wasn't, I knew I was in the clear.

"Where were you earlier?" I asked him with a scowl.

He gave no answer, and I didn't hammer home the point. I tipped his helmet and flew down the escalator. I was back in my little space, before anyone knew anything had happened. It was early to go to bed, and my stomach was rumbling from hunger, but too much had happened. To go back out now would be to risk exposing myself. I would have to go to bed hungry.

I was getting ready to pull the blankets up over me, to look once more at my passport and my ticket, to remind myself who I was, and to think of the future. I didn't get the chance.

There was a push on the paneling that made an entryway. The space may have been a closet once, but there was no door to be found now. The panel left only a small space to fit through, I always had to push it just the right way to get it to open properly.

Whoever was pushing on it now had no such knowledge.

The person would push, have no success, and push again with the same result. But the persistent intruder kept pushing in certain spaces, and the paneling began to give way. This person was starting to figure out how to get inside.

There was nothing I could do. If I tried to push back, then I'd put myself in direct danger from the intruder. So, I pulled all my things as close to me as possible and crouched into the farthest corner, which was just five feet away from the entrance. I could only wait and wonder who it was trying to get in. Was it a guard who had seen me crawl inside? Was it a kid who had found my home by accident?

I didn't have to wait long to find out. Within moments, I saw the dirty blonde hair of the woman peeking through. She was a persistent one. With great effort, she squeezed inside, somehow not ripping her dress, and sat in the corner opposite from me, as she caught her breath.

"What in the world," she said, as she looked around the room.

She saw old wrappers of stolen food, books I had borrowed from the gift shop, deodorant I had used to try and hide my smell, and all the blankets and sweatshirts that were my bed and pillow. Then, she saw me, huddled into a corner like a whipped dog.

"You . . . what . . . ," was all she managed to say.

"Please leave," I said, barely managing to speak in more than a whisper.

"You need to explain yourself," she said, still confused but trying to sound commanding.

"No, I don't," I replied, just as fast. "I don't know you."

The woman huffed out a laugh.

"I thought I was your mother," she said.

I couldn't tell if this woman was being sarcastic or actually believed she was my mother.

"You're a stranger," I said. "I shouldn't have used you, but I want nothing more to do with you. Please, go away."

I couldn't remember who had told me, but I was never to speak to strangers. Strangers couldn't be trusted. Whether this woman understood that, I was not sure, because even after I said so, she still didn't leave.

"What is that smell?" she asked.

I didn't smell anything.

The glazed look that swept over her eyes seemed to confirm that I was the source of the smell.

"Look," she said. "Why don't you come out from there, and we'll talk."

She started to inch closer, extending her hand, as if she expected me to take it as easily as I had before. A part of me wanted to. It had been comforting to have someone to fall back on, but I couldn't take it again. She was going to take me away, away from PIT.

"No," I shouted.

For a moment, I feared the entire building had heard my scream. It was the loudest noise I had ever made. This was the most frightened I had ever been. No one came to inspect the noise, but the woman was stunned by it. She stopped as still as Franco or Rex. If her goal was not to frighten me, she had failed, and she understood that.

She fell back into the corner and remained there for several moments. She seemed to be waiting for something. Waiting for me to calm down, maybe.

After some time, she started digging around in her satchel. She didn't carry a purse. She pulled out a wallet, a thin one, and her passport. She slid one foot closer, holding up her free hand to show that she meant peace, and tossed them to me.

She gestured for me to pick them up, and I did. It may have been a trick, but I was curious what her game was. I picked them up, but as I ran my fingers through them, I kept the woman in my view.

Inside the wallet, I found a handful of ID cards. The woman's name was Lindsay Farris. She owned a Wisconsin driver's license but had a badge from Pittsburgh General Hospital. The badge said she worked as a children's surgeon. Was I supposed to be comforted by that knowledge?

This woman, Lindsay, didn't say anything. She would look at me from time to time and smile, as if she were doing everything possible to show that she meant no harm.

I kept looking through her ID cards, somewhat afraid what might happen if I stopped looking. To prolong the moment, I tossed her my passport. For several moments, we remained like this, each trying to learn as much as possible about the other without saying a word. I was determined not to be the one to break the silence.

"So, Rose Conner," Lindsay said. "If that's what you'd like me to call you. Pleasure to meet you."

I took my time responding to her. I couldn't think of what to say. I couldn't remember the last time that had happened.

"What do you want?" I managed to ask.

"Well, I wanted to know who the strange girl who just kicked me in the shins was," she replied. "Now that I'm here, that question has become much more elaborate."

"You could've just called a guard."

"I suppose I could've, if I thought you were a threat. But just then, and right now, all I see is a scared little girl."

"The best thing for you to do . . . is leave."

"Why is that?"

"Because I don't like you looking at me."

This wasn't totally true. There were worse-looking people. It was more the fact that anyone was looking at me at all, looking at me and this room no one was supposed to know about it. If I was going to get home, then my hiding space had to remain a secret.

Lindsay glanced down at her phone. She was checking the time. She sighed and looked up at the ceiling, before turning her gaze back to me.

"Rose, my job is to help people who can't help themselves. People who need help getting back on their feet."

"I was doing fine, before you showed up. I'm not suffering."

"Before I showed up, you were about to be dragged off to the holding room."

"I would've gotten away."

"No, you wouldn't have."

"What do you care?"

My outburst caught her off guard, but only for a moment.

"When I see someone in need, I can't sit idly by," Lindsay said.

She was righteous, this one. More important, she appeared to be telling the truth.

I didn't respond. I was hoping she'd go away. I knew that this would all lead nowhere the moment she turned the pages of my passport and found the boarding pass. By now, she had probably noticed that the port of arrival was not listed as Pittsburgh.

"This is a very old photo in the passport, Rose. How do I know it's you?" Lindsay asked.

What? How could she say that? Of course it was me. I couldn't remember not having it on me. The passport was mine. The photo proved as much. It looked just like me. At least, I thought it did.

Lindsay reached over to hand the passport, open to the picture page, to me. She also held out her phone. Her phone had a camera on it that allowed me to see myself. I looked at myself in the phone, and I looked at the photo in the passport. What I saw were two little girls, separated by at least six years, with some similarities but nothing outstanding. I couldn't say for certain that the two girls were the same person.

I could not manage to utter words, only sounds. I think I was crying.

"Rose," Lindsay said.

It was then that I realized she had scooted to the middle of the space. I didn't cower. The look on her face expressed concern. I wanted to believe the feeling was genuine.

"Where are your parents?" Lindsay asked.

Gloucester. That was the answer. It was always the answer. That's what my passport said. If they had lost me, that's where they'd be.

Or was it Singapore? That's what the boarding pass said. Did they think I was there?

"I don't know," I answered.

"Well, where is your home?" Lindsay asked.

Just say something, anything to satisfy this woman, I told myself. The confusion was insufferable. It hurt.

Nothing came out. All I managed to do was look around. I knew this place better than anyone. I knew of its forgotten rooms and secret doors. I knew the voices of the workers who came in and out. The scent of the people passing through was comforting.

Rex. Franco. The people here. They never left. They were forever. They didn't lose people. I could picture all of their faces in a moment. But my parents—

"PIT," I finally said.

"Pitt? Pittsburgh?" Lindsay asked, inquisitively.

I shook my head. "PIT. P.I.T."

A look of realization passed over her. Then, she began scrummaging around the blankets, digging through countless food wrappings and perfume bottles. She could see it. She could see the room. My bedroom. All around her was the black and gold of PIT.

"Rose, how long have you been here?" she asked.

I couldn't say. I'd forgotten. I reached out my hand. She understood what I wanted. She gave me back the boarding pass. I looked at the date on it.

"However long it's been since that day," I said, before handing back the piece of paper. I had suddenly lost all connection I had felt with it.

"Four years?" she asked. Hers was not an angry exclamation, but one of shock. "You've been living like this for four years?"

"If you say so," I answered, hiding my surprise at the length of time.

"How?"

"PIT has everything I need. I can take what's necessary. No one notices you when you're four feet tall."

Lindsay was about to ask another question, but I was making my way to the door.

"I'm not trying to run. I just need some air. I'm not used to having another person in here. You can follow me, if you must."

Lindsay nodded her head, and together, we stepped out into the hall.

Something had changed. Rex was no longer the ferocious protector he had once been. He was little more than a pile of bones. I laughed. He was just like I always said he was to frightened children.

The same was true of Franco. He appeared pale, now. Too solid. His body was unnaturally bent; whereas, George looked tall and regal.

Even the airplane hanging from the ceiling was little more than a toy for giants.

I walked without purpose. Lindsay remained close behind.

Everything we passed was familiar but different, somehow.

I stopped at the seat that looked out over the runway. It was the same place I sat, whenever I was looking for a lost wallet. Here, I would look out at Pittsburgh and wonder why anybody ever came here.

"You never tried to leave?" Lindsay asked, taking a seat next to me, mirroring how we had first found each other.

"And go where? There's nothing but mountains and wilderness out there," I said, gesturing toward the window.

Lindsay sighed, as if I had missed some crucial detail.

"That can't be the only reason. Weren't you trying to get onto a plane?"

Blind hope. That was the true reason. If I couldn't get back to mama and papa, then I had to hope they'd get back to me. I had to hope they'd trace their steps and find their way back. If I left, they'd never find me.

"I can't leave."

"Can't leave? What are you talking about?"

"They lost me here. If I stay, they'll come back, eventually. If they lost me here, they know I'm here."

"Rose," Lindsay said, putting her hand on my shoulder.

"No, you can't trust strangers. Can't rely on anyone else. You get lost, you stay where you are."

"Who told you that?"

"Someone from before. Before PIT."

I felt dizzy. Nothing was making sense. Everything was spinning. I couldn't even think of my own name. It was there, in front of me but always just beyond my grasp. The world didn't know who I was, and I had forgotten, too.

The sun was setting in the distance. The airport lights switched on, accordingly.

"Don't you have a plane to catch?" I said, sniffling.

Lindsay pulled out her phone and started pressing buttons.

"I did," she answered. "But then I got this alert that my flight was forced to land in Phoenix, due to bad weather. It won't be here until the morning, and then I have a whole day of flying in front of me."

Lindsay held the phone out to me, as if to prove she wasn't lying. She wasn't, though my eyes were drawn more to her destination than the fact that it was delayed. She was connecting with a flight in Los Angeles that was headed for Melbourne, Australia.

My mind wandered to the digital advertisements of this place. Sunny beaches, smiling people, wild animals. It looked like a paradise. A paradise on the opposite side of the world.

"Why so far away?" I asked.

"My husband. He's already there. Teaching."

"Why didn't you go with him?"

"I had to finish my contract at the hospital and then find a place that would hire me down there."

"I assume you did find a job."

"Very astute of you."

"And it's just—" I began

"Just the two of us," Lindsay finished. "No kids to speak of. Not for lack of trying."

Lindsay laughed, but I didn't understand why.

"Why, you want to come with me?" she asked all of a sudden.

"No," I said instinctively.

But now I was thinking about it. To go to a place of sunshine, to leave behind the cold and the snow. Could I leave PIT? Could I leave behind the only place I could remember? All the things here that were familiar to me?

"I mean, you couldn't buy me a ticket," I said. "That'd be too much money."

"True. It would be a lot. But I'm involved now."

"What?"

"Rose, I won't drag you out of here kicking and screaming. That wouldn't solve anything, but I can't leave here without helping you."

"Helping me?"

No one had ever offered to help me. If anything, I was the one who helped people. I helped the kids that Rex would scare, helped the old ladies up the escalator, helped the gift shop clerk lay off unwanted snacks. No one helped me. No one notices you when you're four feet tall.

"What do you mean?" I asked.

"I can't let you go back to that closet. You're sleeping in filth, and you look anemic. I can't leave knowing you won't be taken care of."

"So, what happens now?"

Lindsay didn't have a direct answer. The two of us sat together like this for several minutes, watching planes lift off into the sky.

Lindsay chuckled to herself.

"I can't believe I'm about to do this," she said.

I looked up at her, still confused.

"I'm prepared to cancel my ticket and go into Pittsburgh with you. If you are Rose Conner, we might be able to track down where your parents went."

I supposed I wasn't born at PIT, so someone had to know who I was. That was comforting, but it also angered me. I was angry at myself for doubting who I was, after all this time.

"Or," Lindsay continued, "and this is the more drastic decision, you could come with me to Australia. We need to try and figure out who you really are."

I was Rose Conner, and I lived at PIT. It didn't matter if I was from Gloucester, like my passport said, or if I was headed to Singapore, like the boarding pass said. PIT was my home, and Rose Conner was my name. Of course, all that hinged on whether the passport and boarding pass actually were mine.

But now, Lindsay was offering to take me to the opposite side of the world.

"You could do that?" I asked.

She nodded. "Of course. You were born, so you're on record."

I considered the truth of these words.

Then, she said, "Someone out there knows who you are."

Craig Czury

SEA NOTES

For Heather

I. BAY OF FUNDY

In all its chaos
grassy salt beach stone
in all its spiritual cluster of white caps
evening before our first voyage
we are imitating the sea blindfolded
led out onto a cliff

We are imitating the full moon
burning through fog
blindfolded
led into the woods
skirting the kidney-shaped tide pool
between sea and sky
a game I don't really understand
ageless   navigating the rocks

I hear someone walking behind me

II. KAYAK

Now my body extends
across the surface of the sea
as with everywhere else
I need to find balance

III. Fin Whales

You show us
that part of you
we have most in common
spouting intermittently
between deeper thoughts

Your presence
stirs something primal in me
I really want to see your face

Something else forgotten
I stare for you
across the horizon
to remind me

IV. Sailing into the Soup

Even more dramatic
rising above the surface
what we think we see

V. Wind and Salt and Sea

I want to figure out something basic
—source of wind

I want to figure out
this timeless species of wind
—salt

I need to fathom
the salt wind of my lungs
when I breathe underwater

VI. FROM WHISTLE LIGHTHOUSE
When the minke whale rolls and dives
when the harbor seal bobs and dives
when my next thought breaches and dives
the moon is in total control

VII. AT SEA
Buoy bell clangs at sunset
—church

VIII. LOST & FOUND AT SEA
Found at sea
one all encompassing fog
one mighty wind
infinite swells with monstrous white caps

Lost at sea
predilection toward sleepwalking

IX. SCHOOL
These forty-some years later
something vaguely heard
immediately blown-off
in a classroom
sets its hook and bam
I suddenly get it

x. Full Moon

I could have walked out to you
on your beam across the sea
I would have
if the one I love
wasn't here inside me

xi. Coriolis Effect

Again as a planet we're spinning
and again I have to take your word for it

Even the water has its doubts

xii. Burial at Sea

Scent of roses
blown in with the tide

Oh yes
this is a very bad sign

Someone out there
has been cast off with garlands

xiii. Machias Seal Island

Agéd eye
innocent eye
tired concerned
weary eye
old and sympathetic
eyes of the puffin

XIV. BUT

Where did they go
the low tide dulse men
the herring smoke-fingered women

Where did they go
with that brine fog look in their eyes

gull skree   tide pool

XV. BEYOND THE PINES

Fishcrow raven screeches
swallowed by fog
a foreboding *aaaehhh*
repeated *aaaehhh*

Imagine hearing a baby crying
out there
a woman on the cliff giving birth

XVI. PHOSPHORESCENCE

There's a dark corner of the sea
where angels blurt the sins of drowned sailors
—phosphorescent

XVII. WHITEHEAD ISLAND

Sea and wind smooth these rocks
the sun bakes   bleaches white
until they hatch and fly away
the air swarming salt crystals in its beaks

XVIII. LIQUID HAIKU

I amm tryyyinnng
to sayyy somethinnng tooo youuuu
whoaaaaaa

XIX. YOU

I am watching you stretch
your fingers this wide
across a maritime map
of rock and sand

You expect no one
separate from the sea
and you're singing
as close as I am to you
walking out to greet you

XX. EITHER

She really wasn't dead
or I buried the wrong cat

Either way four nights later
she came back scratching the screen door
I went down to where I buried her
but the tide was in and her grave
was under water

XXI. HOLD FAST

Tangled spindle drift I blow through
like a police whistle

No one arrests the full moon
and the crimes of the sea
go unpunished

XXII. AGAINST THE CLIFF

With what washes ashore in the tides
I could build my house

With what blows in on the wind
I could build my song

You could build your song
with that long weathered scar
above your eye

Wind disintegrates into sea

XXIII. IN THIS CLIMATE

You could get a lot of writing done
if you didn't have to
fuss around with all these words

XXIV. TELL ME

What has the sea failed
the wind
the gulls gannets cormorants loons
ghostly cloak of fog

The fish know where the bottom is
and the sea goes there
to retreat regroup   re-salting its revenge

XXV. ASHBURTON HEAD
At this height
such vast undulating blue sea
I have also experienced
in Umbria
among the rolling umber amber ochre hills
so alive and vibrant with the unknown
—a picnic table painted

XXVI. LEAVING THE ISLAND
Each of us has his own sadness
her own sadness

I know I have my own but it's secret
possibly from a place long before I was born
only it intensifies when I'm leaving
not thinking about leaving
not packing to leave
but in motion
which also could be a sadness for arriving
this secret excitement I have for becoming no one

—Grand Manan Island, New Brunswick, Canada
July, 2005

Alexander Mercant

OBSESSION

CHESS IS WAR. Anyone who says otherwise should have no place at the table. They do not deserve to hold the pieces in their hands. They have no mind necessary to command the battle across the board, like the great generals of history: Alexander, Hannibal, Ghengis, Zhukov. Men who truly understood sacrifice. It is no wonder to me that humans fight to the death. There is no worse feeling in the world than defeat and no glory greater than that of victory—to scan the table, to analyze it all, to see it in your mind, the pieces standing firm and still under your complete control, and to execute, with perfect precision, a linear and logical series of moves you have created.

On this particular day, he opened with a gambit, a gambit I gracefully accepted, sweeping his piece off the table. This was a war of two men, of two minds, the minds that decide the fate of the wooden lives under their fingertips. Great men always control the lives of lesser men. My legacy and legend do not belong in the soggy fields of the French countryside, the winters of Russia, or the hammering of a siren or a microphone, with men scrambling to find their helmets, rifles, and courage. They belong wherever the war takes me. At the table, holding my own.

My men stand strong, completely obedient to the hand guiding them to greatness. Whether that is found in life or death matters little. I can hear the breathing of the audience to my left. I know there are thousands watching from the television and on the Internet, but they are no more than buzzards flying over Gettysburg.

I make my move.

He makes his.

I put my hand to my chin and think. The future is decided by the superior mind, like the minds of the men who came before me. The camera creeks, zooming in, watching as my hand picks up a knight. My horse jumps over a pawn and lands a fork, an outstretched arm with sword swiping at two pieces. What a humiliating trap for him to be caught in, like a child soldier with a pinless grenade.

I think of the money for a moment, not that it ever mattered to me. It's just that this is the largest winnings pot for a chess game in history. Not that I need it. I don't require much more than victory and vodka, which brings my mind for a moment to the hotel room bar with its little bottles of booze, like chess pieces lined up for the taking.

I lean back in my chair.

My opponent's eyes are scanning the table and forming a counter-attack, a way to set me back on my heels. His fears are like generals, in their war tent, looking to turn the tide.

He moves again.

I move right away. My mind is steps ahead of his. My men are frothing at the mouth, thirsty for blood.

He blunders. His men are afraid, pressed up against one another, tripping to their doom.

I almost laugh at my genius. We might as well put the board away and give me my money.

He moves, trying to take the center.

I move back, a mistake planned.

He's desperate to get ahead. He sacrifices a piece to leave his bishop pinned.

Then, he gets up from the table to walk.

I look over at the audience. Someone is holding a video camera. I wonder how I look but decide I don't care.

When he sits down, he plays one of the three moves I'd imagined him choosing.

I return to my attack, and I know it's over. My men stand strong. His side of the board is a display of men fleeing for their lives; no organization, no structure, a lazy mess of men better off dead.

My white pieces have invaded, filled with blood-lust, ready to hack off their heads and throw the corpses from this world to the floor. I spend my next three moves cleaning up the board.

The sweat on my opponent's brow grows thicker by the piece. When he makes a good move, I don't even acknowledge it and continue on with what I've planned. One man can always die for the rest. It is in our nature.

When I slide down with my queen hitting the F7 square, I know he does have one move to counter me, for it isn't something he'd anticipated. When he fails to counter, I almost burst out laughing across the table.

It's mate in four. My men served well. The war will be won.

He stands up again, and while he walks around the table like a warhorse looking for a way out of death, I remember the places this game has taken me. Trophies, books, and signings. Things I smile and do because that's what we are supposed to do. It's our role. I am no different than Churchill, Stalin, and Roosevelt at Yalta.

Like a knight that hooks, a bishop that slides, or a king that staggers, we all play our part, our role, our position. Mine is to be perfect. It is in our nature from the moment we are carved from the immaterial, the same as wood—as brittle as wood, as well-defined as any chess piece.

Most humans want to make it to the endgame, to make themselves grandmasters of their lives, but there are blunders. There are sacrifices. People go down to protect one another, and plenty resign before the pieces of life go back into the box. My game is short, but I play it with excellence. There would be no point in a play, if not in the pursuit of perfection, and I am always perfect.

When my opponent sits back down, he surprises me. Not in a way that would save his life. Just enough to give him a line of hope.

A hope I crush, as his rook is removed from the board.

I would have imagined he'd resign, but he stays on. Sportsmanship or suicide?

Is it better to die before defeat? I would not know.

I give him a quick death.

Checkmate.

A word.

A sound.

As powerful as the Soviet Anthem playing in Berlin on May 2, 1945.

I stand. The audience stands. It's what I've come to know. I reach my hand across the table and shake his. Mine is as dry as the board, his as wet as the water on the stand.

Good game. Good game.

It takes longer than I want, but I receive my check. My photo is taken, and my car pulls up out front. Reporters who barely know an opening or the history of this art form try to ask me questions. They want to know what it takes, how I got to where I am, and what I plan to do. They always want to know how I am going to spend the money.

It's always the money, but it's never about the money to me. My name will be in the history books of this game. I want to live forever, immortal like the men I admire.

I sit back in the rental car and breathe in the smell of fresh leather. My driver already knows where to take me. I see the city lights off to the side, as we drive.

Plenty of people are out. I imagine them drinking away, dancing under the starlight, the bars pouring shots and filling glasses, people staggering home.

I walk into my hotel room and flip on the lights. The little pieces have been waiting for me. I walk to the counter and look at them. I make the same move I always do. I empty the vodka bottles into a disposable coffee cup.

I undress and sit down on the couch.

The AC chills my naked body.

The cup is in my right hand. I drink from it.

I flick off the lights.

The room is dark and quiet, but for the murmur of the air conditioning.

I close my eyes.

Now, I'm alone with the board.

A single light, dangling from the ceiling of my imagination, illuminates the board. Perfect shadows extend from the bodies of the soldiers. Their faces are expertly sculpted from the finest marble. There is no one else but me and them. They are ready. They do not know where they will move. I promise them nothing but glory. I take a drink and think, because I have work to do.

I move for one side and then the other.

The carved pieces do not question whether they will live or die.

Thomas Piekarski

HELLO MENDOCINO

It's early morning, the entire North Central Coast
wrapped in a thick fog. Driving the highway,
you must use your wipers. Fort Bragg merchants,
just beginning to open. A cold ocean breeze has
the few browsers bundled up. Sunlight barely pierces
heavy overcast. The small downtown, a tourist venue:
its 20's vintage shops dolled up and well-stocked.
Some crazy lady hollers out in the middle
of the street. Good thing there isn't much traffic.

She's denouncing incoherently, shoots me a glance,
but I stay well away from her and proceed
on my stroll of the past-present. I circle
to the oceanfront, to the Skunk Train depot.
There's that crazy woman again—livid,
standing in front of the sign of a giant skunk.
No doubt it's time to make my getaway. Five miles
down the coast, I pass an impeccable botanical garden,
enter the cradle of the only place to go, Mendocino.

Meanness isn't to be found in Mendocino.
If your computer crashed, and you didn't back up
those priceless files, you may need Mendocino.
When your ego pops like a helium balloon,
and life in the city makes you feel mostly apish,
Mendocino will show you what it means to be human.

There is no graft, no flimsy excuse, no fear found
in Mendocino. Its private headland isolation,
bound to balance you with nature, will nurture
body and spirit. Solidarity, oneness, kinetic energy,
instant gratification, grand notions, secret revelation,
and inspired strategy are extracted from
the brisk sea air and damp fog that swaddle
the village. I arrive mid-morning

amid the iconic Victorian, Cape Cod,
and Edwardian dwellings; the specialty stores,
fragrant roses, orchids, magnolias, and hyacinth;
charming eateries, ocean vistas and cliffs of Mendocino.

Hareendran Kallinkeel

DOUGH FOR BREAD, DOUGH FOR BUSINESS

RETURNING FROM HIS TWENTY-FIFTH JOB INTERVIEW, exhausted by an hour-long bus journey, Sidharth slumps down onto a sofa.

His father, an Indian Administrative Service officer, has forbidden him to use the car. "Such comforts," according to him, "aren't for young men, with an engineering degree, who cannot find a job."

As if it were Sidharth's fault. In a nation, where universities award degrees liberally without ensuring the quality of academic content, millions graduate every year. Those with some political clout, or funds to pay bribes, get into government jobs; others take up petty jobs in private companies that offer a pittance. Most remain unemployed.

An idealist, his father doesn't accept or pay bribes; nor will he knock at any politician's door. So, Sidharth knows he cannot hope to get a job in the foreseeable future.

Hungry, he goes into the kitchen and finds a loaf of bread. He tears off its wrapper, pulls out a slice. The coarse bread triggers an idea.

"DAD, I'VE THOUGHT OF A BUSINESS."

His father looks at him for a long moment. "What business?"

"Bread. People eat it daily. Good quality will bring steady demand."

There has rarely been an occasion when his father has agreed with him.

"Okay, only on one condition."

"Yes, Dad."

"You have ten minutes," his father says, with a pronounced sneer, with absolute certainty that his son won't be able to meet his challenge. "Tell me in three words. What are the two most important things you need for a bread business?"

Sweat drenching his forehead, Sidharth listens to his heart pound.

His father consults his watch. "Eight—"

Sidharth takes a long breath. "Raise the dough."

For the first time in years, a benevolent smile lights up his father's face. "Son," he says, "you should be writing flash fiction."

Daniel de Leon

WALLS OF FIRE

AT AGE FIVE, KEAHI RAN THROUGH WALLS OF FIRE.

"That's my boy," said his father Afi, rooted in their native tongue. Afi snuffed torches with a bare hand. Now, he grabbed his son in both arms and kissed the top of the boy's head. "You'll be the greatest fire-dancer that this island has ever seen."

They returned, through the trails that coursed the island, to their hut, with Afi's arm slung around the boy's shoulders.

When his mother served supper that evening, Keahi pulled at her skirt and asked, "Can't I go to the show?"

She replied, as she always did, "One day."

Keahi awoke every morning with the feeling that his mother's "one day" would not be today. Undeterred, he asked his question each evening at supper, until "one day" arrived.

"Can I go to the show tonight?"

"Stay safe," she replied.

Keahi lit up and ran through the hut. He hugged his mother and begged his father to leave immediately, before she changed her mind.

As they headed out the door of the hut, Keahi's mother gripped Afi's hand with a strength he had never known the woman to possess. "If one spark so much as touches that boy, I'll have your eyeballs in a stew before morning."

Afi nodded. "On my eyes."

"And another thing," she said. "No booze tonight."

"You've brought the boy?" Tanaki did a double-take.

It's his time," Afi said.

Tanaki called to his wife. His own son, Maleko, would join them that evening, as well.

The men set up the stage on the beach at dusk. When the final flecks of sun faded from the sky, Afi and Tanaki sat their sons in the back, by the bar, far from their sand-built stage.

"I want to go to the front," Keahi said.

The front is for the *haoles*," Afi responded. "We need the white people up front, so that they can tip."

"But we can't see from here."

"If you want to come back again, you won't move from that spot," Afi said.

A crowd gathered around the stage on the starlit beach. Tanaki began to beat his drum. Afi lit both ends of a baton, twirling it slowly to the rhythm of Tanaki's percussion. As Afi circled, the tourists gravitated from the bar and the shore to watch the man who danced with fire. Keahi took it in—the rhythm, the footwork, the white people clapping and shouting over the beat, and his father, his idol, controlling the crowd and the fire with godly command.

To stay seated required all of the boy's strength, as he watched his father juggle flaming knives and swallow fiery torches. He had observed his father and Tanaki rehearsing in the jungle, but he had never seen the flame spinning before the star-speckled sky on the beach, where not a soul stirred, everyone transfixed by the roar and the light, by the sweat, glowing as it dripped down the torso of Afi, the master of fire.

By age six, Keahi no longer needed his mother's permission to go to the show. She often asked Afi to leave the boy at home, but Keahi and Maleko had become part of the act. The owner of the bar, an American named Bill, paid the boys a nightly stipend to walk through the crowds on the beach with a bottle in tow, pouring shots for white tourists at double the price. At the end of each show, when Afi completed his finale, both Keahi and Maleko would move through the crowd, hats in hand to press the tip money from tourists.

Then, one night, following a silent supper in their hut, his mother said, "Keahi stays with me tonight."

Afi dropped his spoon hard against the table. "Where is this coming from?"

"I'm tired of feeling worry every time you leave the hut. This is how you earn your living, Afi, and I'm grateful, but I cannot accept this for Keahi."

"I need him," Afi said. "Keahi, tell Mama how much money you took in with the hat last night."

"Forty dollars," Keahi said.

"Forty dollars," Afi said. "I can't get that on my own—When people see the boy, they understand. It's the only way these *haoles* give us tips."

Keahi imagined juggling flaming knives on a moonlit beach, as tears formed in his mother's tired eyes.

"We've scraped by on less in the past," she said. "I'd pay forty dollars not to feel this worry, anymore."

"We're running late, my beautiful. Rest, and you'll feel better," Afi said.

"I cannot rest," she said, her voice tight.

Keahi stared at her.

"You're not listening, Afi. If you take him tonight, I am leaving."

"Calm yourself, my queen," Afi soothed her. We'll talk in the morning. The sun is nearly set. We need to go, now."

"On my eyes," she said, "I'll leave this damned island."

Afi gripped his wife by the shoulders. His voice was firm. "You need the boy to do these shows, if you want to have the cash to leave."

Then, Afi released her. He shut the door and led his boy to meet Tanaki and Maleko.

THAT NIGHT, AFI PUT ON THE SHOW of his life. He performed every trick as if it were his last, in perfect rhythm with Tanaki, the two of them conjoined at the soul. The crowd of *haoles* grew with each flicker of the flame, from the fire of the yo-yo to the juggling of flaming blades. Afi juggled two knives, as Tanaki played the drum. Keahi no longer passed the hat. Now, he dipped a rag in gasoline to wrap the third knife for his father. Tourists gravitated from neighboring beach bars to ogle the performer who twirled a flaming baton with his foot, as he swallowed a flame-engulfed torch.

As Afi climbed the ladder for his grand finale, tourists crowded in, from the bar to the sea. Afi thought not of how many of them there might be, nor of how much tip money awaited. He focused only on the post straight in front of him, as he stepped onto the tightrope. Tanaki pounded the drum, and Keahi tossed his father flaming devil sticks. The rhythm of walking the tightrope must be exact—One missed beat could throw him off.

Afi walked the rope, forwards and backwards, then balanced on one foot, all the while juggling the fire. He zoned in on the post straight ahead, his concentration rising from the chaos, from the life surrounding him.

In that moment, in the center of the circled masses, Afi danced beyond the tourist's flashing cameras, and he touched the night, the primal spirit of the island's heritage. He felt the flames of the first kindled fire. Extinguishing the wicks with his mouth, he tossed the used sticks down to Keahi.

Then, leaping down from the tightrope, Afi offered a dramatic bow. Keahi and Maleko swept the crowd for tip money, moving quickly to reach the whites in the back of the crowd who had already turned to leave for the next bar.

AFI AND TANAKI SAT AT THE BAR, as they always did after a show. Bill, the bar's owner, poured a round of rum. "We've never had a crowd like that in all my years," he said.

As the tourists dispersed through the sands, Keahi and Maleko ran toward their fathers with their hats full of money.

Afi lifted Keahi. He twirled the boy in the night.

"The fire of my life," Afi said, as he kissed his son.

Afi and Tanaki poured the money out onto the bar. They counted it.

Bill poured another round of rum.

"Leave the bottle," Afi said.

"Come on, Afi. Go home to your wife. You did good work tonight," Bill said.

Turning to his son, Afi said, "Look at me, boy. We only drink when the job is done. Never in your life drink on the job."

Bill laughed. "As far as men go, Afi is the most principled drunk you'll ever see."

Afi continued counting the tips. "This can't be," he said, suddenly. He slammed his palm down upon the bar. "Keahi, where is the rest of it?"

Keahi looked back at Afi. "That's what we got."

"Thirty-six dollars? You expect me to believe that's all we got?" Afi smacked his son. "Don't thieve me, boy. We had white people from here to goddamn Canada tonight. Where is the money?"

"I tried, but some people didn't give," Keahi said. He held back tears.

Afi upended the bottle to swig the liquor. He turned to Tanaki. "Take the boys to your hut. Bring them to the clearing in the morning."

Tanaki disappeared with the boys, and Afi turned back to the bottle.

Stumbling into the hut after midnight, he dropped the bottle, now empty. Glass broke across the ground.

FIFTY METERS PAST THE VILLAGE stretched a round treeless patch in the jungle. Afi and Tanaki called this patch of land "the clearing," and they met there for rehearsals, daily. Waiting for Tanaki and the boys, Afi took the time to overcome the liquor that still pounded against his temples. He imagined how he'd handle his wife, when he returned to their hut.

Tanaki and Keahi arrived.

"Where's Maleko?" Afi asked.

"He didn't want to come, today," Tanaki said.

"He's a child. What does it matter what he wants?"

"He says he wants to go to school. He wants, one day, to study in an American college."

"The only thing America can teach our people is how to act like monkeys," Afi said. He turned to Keahi. "And you? Do you want to go to school?"

"No," Keahi said.

Afi mussed his son's hair. "That's a good boy. It's time we teach you to dance—Do you agree?"

Keahi nodded.

Afi drew a wooden blade from his bag and handed it to the boy.

"Do as I do," he instructed.

Afi soaked a towel in fuel. He wrapped it tightly around his metal blade. Keahi followed suit with his own wooden blade.

Tanaki lit the towels up in flames, and Afi tossed his flaming blade from hand to hand.

Keahi juggled the wooden blade well, but this was his first time tossing fire. He felt the heat transfer between his two hands, until it became too intense to bear. On the fifth toss, he let the flaming wood fall to the ground.

Afi stooped. Lifting the fiery wood from the dirt, he crouched before his son. Keahi reached out to take the blade, but Afi grabbed his son's hand. He pressed the fiery knife into Keahi's naked forearm. Keahi's skin smoldered. He tried to pulled his arm away, but his father's grip overpowered him.

Tanaki moved to separate Keahi from his father.

"Keep out of this, Tanaki," Afi said.

Keahi felt the pain, but he didn't wail.

Afi lifted the blade from his son's arm, maintaining his vice-like grip on the boy's hand. "You think that I'm unkind, teaching you a lesson like this," Afi said, "but fire will be far more unkind and less forgiving."

KEAHI WORRIED ALL DAY ABOUT what he'd tell his mother about the flesh that had blistered on his arm, but when he and his father arrived at their home, she was gone. His mother had vacated the hut.

Afi promised his son that she would return the next day, but she did not—nor did she surface the day after that.

Maleko continued to attend the fire show each night to help Keahi gather tips from the *haoles*, but Keahi arrived at the clearing alone to rehearse with his father and Tanaki, each day.

Maleko graduated from one school-year to the next, while Keahi advanced from juggling to eating fire. At the end of each day, Keahi arrived at the hut with new blisters and burns in his mouth.

"You must tolerate the pain," Afi told his son one evening, as they supped on stew in their hut. "I remember when I was your age and I learned to eat fire—the constant blisters on my tongue, my lips, my throat. But you won't see those blisters in my mouth, today. You won't even see the scars they left."

Keahi nodded. It hurt too much to speak.

"I bet you can't taste a single flavor in the stew."

Keahi nodded, once again.

"Neither can I. Your mother should have taught you how to cook."

Keahi wanted to say that his mother should still be here, that it was Afi's fault that he could taste nothing, that he wanted to attend school but couldn't, that he felt imprisoned by four walls of fire, but it hurt too much to speak, so Keahi only nodded.

BY AGE EIGHT, KEAHI WAS PERFORMING in his father's shows. Maleko still passed the hat for tips, but Keahi didn't get many tips.

"Earn the tip," Afi told his son. "No one will give it to you."

He did earn the tip, Keahi thought, but the white people withheld it.

"Stop treating *haoles* as friends," Afi said. "They act like they are, of course, but they are not your friends."

In time, Keahi earned better tips. As the boy grew, Tanaki's role diminished, and Maleko quit attending their shows altogether, favoring his nightly studies. Raking sand between shows on the beach, Keahi asked his father, "Why doesn't Maleko have to eat fire?"

"Maleko's a white-worshipper," Afi said.

"But he used to come to shows with me. We both used to come, and then Maleko got to go to school."

"You don't want to go to school."

"I think I might."

Afi smacked him. "Focus, Keahi. I've never had an accident, and I refuse to have one tonight."

In the second show that night, Keahi danced for the white people, building suspense with every toss and twirl of the fiery knives and torches.

An impressive crowd gathered to watch Afi perform the grand finale on his tightrope. Afi stumbled three times on the rope, but the show ended without incident.

Keahi and Tanaki gathered tips in their upturned hats. Keahi brought the tips to his father.

"Twenty-six dollars," Afi groaned. He dropped his head onto the bar.

Bill left the bottle.

"People say you drink too much," Keahi said.

"I have my principles, and I stick by them," said Afi. "I've never had a drink on the job."

"You're getting slow," said Keahi. "Tell him, Tanaki."

"We're getting old," Tanaki said.

Years rolled forth and crashed like the tide. Keahi's scars faded. He could hardly remember the last time his father had branded him—He had performed for some time now without flaw. Even Afi admitted that, with continued dedication, his son's gift for fire could outgrow his own.

As Keahi's role in Afi's show increased, Keahi began to receive more tips than Tanaki.

When Maleko applied for admission to American schools, Tanaki quit the show altogether. "You have no need for me," he told Afi, "and I no longer have need for you. I put Maleko through school. I bought his books. He won't need me anymore, when he goes to study in America."

Keahi envied Maleko, though they seldom spoke, anymore. They acknowledged each other with nods, when they passed in the street, and all that Keahi knew of Maleko was what his father reported.

"Maleko thinks he's too good for this village," Afi told his son. "He doesn't know that it's no better over in America. Tanaki says his boy has been invited to study at so many places with glorious names—I bet he made it all up."

Keahi eyed his father. Afi's once-chiseled torso spilled over his waistband, as he supped on the *mahi.* In truth, he was slow, always a drink away from having to be hoisted up, though Keahi made sure his sluggard father made it home, each night. The once-imposing figure had changed. Now, his manner, his entitlement, and his yellowed eyes disgusted Keahi.

"Do you ever miss her?" Keahi asked Afi.

"Who?"

"Who do you think?"

"We don't talk about her."

Afi looked toward the bottle beside his mattress.

"Things might be better in America," Keahi said. "But you wouldn't know. You've never gone beyond this village."

"The Americans come and watch you play with fire each night, like you're a clown. They fill their fat bellies and don't tip a penny, and now you defend them."

"Are you drunk?"

"I never drink before a show."

"There's a world outside of this village. That's all I'm saying. You can't blame Maleko for wanting to explore that."

"They're the bad guys, Keahi. Don't you see? They have no culture, no history. They feed on what little we have left. This fire, these dances, they are the only things that tie us to our roots—and you want to forsake this, so that you can be like them?" Afi coughed. He began to choke on the *mahi.*

Keahi slapped his father on the back, until the coughing subsided.

Afi wiped blood from his mouth. "I'm tired," he said.

"You need to rest."

Afi wheezed. "We have a show tonight."

"I can handle it," Keahi said.

"But the tightrope—the finale—"

"I can handle it."

Keahi put his father to bed. As he left for the beach, his father called after him.

"Yes, father."

"Bring a bottle home from Bill."

ON HIS WAY TO THE BEACH, Keahi stopped at Tanaki's, interrupting what appeared to be a family celebration.

"Come in," said Tanaki with joy. "Come celebrate with us. Maleko has accepted an offer to study economics at the University of Illinois."

"Congratulations," Keahi said. He stood bare-chested in flame-resistant leather shorts and stared at Maleko in his collar and tie. He hardly recognized his old friend.

"Dine with us," Maleko said, gesturing toward the ten-pound fish on the table.

"I can't," Keahi said, embarrassed. "I'm sorry to interrupt, but I've come to ask a favor."

"Anything," Tanaki said.

"My father's sick. I need your help with the show, tonight."

Tanaki looked to his son.

AFI'S HEALTH ONLY DECLINED. As Maleko studied economics overseas, Keahi dove into the school of the flame. Afi had been right in teaching his son that the art was to dance and not to perform a series of tricks, but what Afi failed to realize, what Keahi understood, was that the art is more about a beat than the dance. They were performing for a new generation of tourists now, a generation that didn't care or notice what went on under or over the beat, so long as the beat continued to pulse. So, Keahi convinced Bill to upgrade the bar's speaker system. With club beats blaring from the powerful amps, Keahi no longer needed Tanaki.

This new generation of tourists was younger. Their clothing was scanty, and they were touchy—the bikini-clad girls brushed their dainty white hands across Keahi's muscles—but their attention span was short. One beat's pause could lose half the crowd. They needed to feel that they were part of the show.

Every night, Keahi brought a bottle home to his father. The liquor was the only medicine that could get Afi to sleep. Then, one morning, Afi didn't wake up. Keahi felt for his father's heart, no longer beating. A half-empty bottle of rum still sat on the table.

Keahi swigged the bottle, and he spilled a measure out onto the ground beside his father. Looking at Afi's cold body, Keahi thought of the pain that his father had inflicted—the scars from his training, the driving away of his mother, the pressure he placed on Keahi to retrace his own path in life. Keahi thought of the pain, and then he let it go.

NEVER WHILE AFI WAS ALIVE would Keahi have performed with a wooden blade instead of a steel one, but the tourists couldn't tell the difference. Keahi saw no need to take unnecessary risks. A hospital bill would incur a debt that he couldn't pay. While the new generation of tourists was different, they maintained the scant tipping tradition of their elders. Although Keahi performed three shows each night, he still could not afford a change of clothes.

Often, the white women stayed for all three shows. After the finale, the women found Keahi at the bar and got him drunk. The first time Keahi slept with a white woman, he considered it a gift from the gods. When he slept with another the following week, he realized that he embodied something they wanted. He began to infuse a sexual energy into his show, closing each performance with a sweet kiss of fire. He ignited a touch of fuel on the palm of his hand with a vapor pull, creating the effect of blowing fire with his breath, with his lips.

The white women loved it. Even the white men loved it. The thought of Keahi, the dancing black master of fire, possessing their women gave them some sort of thrill. At least once a week, he spent the night with a new woman. He believed that he could live this way, forever.

Once, a white woman introduced Keahi to her friends, who she said had come on holiday from college in the United States.

Keahi smiled. "You must know Maleko," he said.

The tourists couldn't hold back their laughter.

Keahi pressed. "Maleko is a friend of mine. He's from my village."

After a moment of silence, one of the white boys broke. "No, man. Can't say we've met your friend."

Afi's words rang through Keahi's mind—They act like it, of course, but they're not your friends. Keahi never repeated this mistake.

AFTER MONTHS OF SLEEPING IN STRANGE HOTEL BEDS, and sometimes being dismissed upon climax, Keahi found the sex to be empty. The white women wanted him drunk, and he felt he was becoming his father. His relations were never anything more than physical. He could never bring a white woman to his hut, not just because she would feel discomfort, but because it would give the other villagers a reason to continue their gossip about him, even now that his father was dead. Besides, he couldn't fully understand these women, when they spoke. He didn't know them, and they didn't know him.

Still, he never felt himself, when he returned to the village. It was as though the *haoles* had changed him, as though they had broken him off from something he had once known as home.

Going through the motions of the show each night, Keahi no longer studied the flame. He knew the beat by rote. He knew the nature of fire.

Passing through each night, he drowned himself in booze and women, until shows and booze and women seemed to muddle in his mind.

Now, a hundred pairs of eyes focused on him alone. Keahi lit a cigarette with the flaming wick of a spinning baton. He smoked the cigarette down, as he tied a scarf over his eyes. Blind, he spun a flaming chain gripped between his teeth. He was a slave to the beat. The crowd roared, until their clapping drowned out the beat.

Between shows, a group of white people with letters on their tank-tops offered to buy Keahi a drink. They slapped him on the back and welcomed him into their circle. Keahi knew that they were not his friends, but the liquor was free, and they had not given tips. He recalled his father's only principle—Never drink before a show.

Keahi didn't know how he would make it through the next show, and the two shows remaining that night were only the first in a lifetime of shows that awaited.

The white tourists raised their shot glasses to Keahi.

He raised his glass, slammed it down against the bar, closed his eyes, and tossed the liquor down his gullet.

Patrick Pfister

THE TENTH MUSE

She understood virginity
as a state of grace
that had abandoned her.

Desire ate her heart,
and Eros scorched her soul,
yet she slept alone with the moon.

Her passion's fire
consumed an entire island.

No dance, no holy place existed
distant from her heat.

Out of what core issued
her burning,
and into what vessel
would it be quenched?

Hila Amit

JUMANA

HE DIED AT NOON. They called Jumana in the morning, as they were taking him to the hospital, but she lingered so long on the way from Tel Aviv to the north that, by the time she arrived, it was all over.

He was laid to rest, while she was stuck in traffic. They couldn't wait. Islam forbids leaving the body unburied overnight. She had promised her mother that she'd arrive by noon, but the sun was already low, and she was moving at a snail's pace. It had been so long since she had returned home that she was not sure she was ready for it. She prayed for a natural disaster of historic proportions that would put her out of reach for three whole days; three days with no decisions, away from her hometown, as well as from Tel Aviv.

It was almost sunset, when her car entered the sharp curves of Umm al-Fahm. Jumana drove up the steep inclines and narrow alleyways with a confidence she could never quite muster in Tel Aviv. She knew every blind corner and dead end. She knew where you had to stick to the right to avoid the perennial pothole. She drove with a sense of deep familiarity for every pedestrian she saw, for the cramped streets, the absent sidewalks, her left foot hovering over the clutch, ready for the next incline, as if by instinct. She was also familiar with the looks darting her way. She was there in the thick of things, but this place had ceased to be hers.

Every person that passed intoned a sad, deep A-Salam Aleikum at her. She braced herself for the racket of the neighborhood—everybody listening to music, everybody playing soccer in the middle of the road. Any moment now, she'd be home. She could already feel the tell-tale itch, like an allergic reaction. She felt it whenever she was close to her family home, at the back of her neck, along her arms, between her breasts. She would scratch her skin raw. This was yet another reason to stay away.

But when she reached the top of her street, everything was quiet. There were no children playing outside, and no music, either. She drove around the bend and came into full view of her parents' house. Their yard and Samir's adjoining one were shielded by two giant black shades. Garden chairs were piled outside by the wall.

It had been the same, years before, when her grandfather had died. The huge shades; the plastic garden chairs from the event center, delivered on overloaded vans; the portable gas burner, set up in the yard to assist the efforts to feed the guests for three days of mourning; the Azza. She remembered, too, the strict segregation— the men sitting in comfort outside, while the women huddled in the cramped living room, indoors. The younger women were to serve each new guest a small cup of black coffee and a fresh date on a napkin. Every new arrival prompted another round of weeping and commiserations, as well as thousands of sad pecks on the wet cheeks of the immediate family.

Tamara had been to Umm al-Fahm a few times. She visited as Jumana's guest, a "Jewish friend." Tamara, a curly blonde who spoke in Hebrew, attracted a lot of attention in their neighborhood. Jumana's family was eagerly hospitable, when the two of them came for dinner during Ramadan, Eid al-Fitr, or Id al-Adha. With time, however, it became clear that Tamara was not just a friend, and eventually her mother told them to stop coming. She would visit them in Tel Aviv instead.

Once inside the house, she called to tell Tamara the news. No, Jumana wriggled, she didn't need to come. It was too late. Maybe not the next day, either. Honestly, she really shouldn't come at all. There was nothing for her to do, and she'd barely understand anything.

Nonsense, Tamara said. Of course she'd come. Yes, it was too late tonight, especially since she couldn't stay over, but she'd drive out straight from work the next day, and she'd bring Jumana's clothes and toiletries.

Next, Jumana called Ofri. The hospital always sent out a delegation on occasions like these. "Tell them to come in the morning, if that's not too much trouble," Jumana said, unable to say no. At least Tamara and Ofri wouldn't both be there at the same time.

Once, at a work wedding, the three of them had all been seated together, and it was unbearable. The host had tried to seat Tamara next to Ofri, with Jumana in the middle, but Jumana had switched seats, made Tamara sit between them. She remembered the dowdy placemats and how Ofri had shot suggestive glances at her over the rice and fried chicken. Her hands shook, so that she'd spilled a bit of her wine. She'd felt like she was sitting on a bomb. She remembered Tamara's dress, too—a sexy red—and how, an hour before they left for the wedding, she had ripped the tag out and stuck her hand down Tamara's panties. Sex was soothing; it pushed Ofri out of her mind.

When the ceremony was over and the music started, she and Tamara got up to dance. They danced close, Jumana with her back to the table. She didn't want to see Ofri looking at her. Still, as she was spinning Tamara around, the music and the lights worked their magic on her like fireworks, and she gave in to Tamara's touch, to how she held her.

Tamara, drunk, whispered to her. Where would their wedding be? In Umm al-Fahm or Tamara's hometown? Tuxedos or gowns? "I see kebabs squashed on giant skewers. I see chocolate cakes and baklava with honey and pistachio," Tamara giggled into her ear. "And I see your father there."

The light reflecting from Ofri's necklace blinded Jumana, and the spell was broken. She wanted to go home.

JUMANA STOOD OUTSIDE WITH THE OTHER WOMEN, waiting for her mother and the men to arrive from the cemetery. Samir's truck turned into their driveway, the passenger's side door opened, and her mother's foot wandered out, searching for the ground. Her right hand clasped a used tissue, while her left grabbed the side of the truck for support. She couldn't see Jumana through her teary eyes.

Ya binti, ya rab, Nasreen mumbled as Jumana fell into her arms, weeping, holding her like she never had before. The world faded away. Jumana saw nothing but her mother. Her eyes were dry. She'd secretly wished for her father's death for more than a decade.

Samir was only a year older than Jumana, and although they'd grown up side-by-side, crawled and breastfed together, he was the eldest son. He stayed in Umm al-Fahm, built himself a house, got married and had kids, while she distanced herself and moved light-years away from home.

She'd distanced herself because of him. He had their father's eyes and imperious voice. He acted as if he were born into their parents' generation, as if he'd been sucked into a premature and miserable adulthood, before he'd quite managed to be a child. He acted as if he had nothing in common with Jumana or with the rest of them, seven brothers and sisters in all.

She remembered how their father had doted on him, how her parents had lavished him with nice clothes and the truck, how they had given him his own private suite in the basement, while she and the others were packed into two cramped rooms, one for the boys and one for the girls. Whenever Samir called out, her mother would hurry down bearing a tray loaded with coffee and cookies.

She walked her mother into the living room and sat her down on the big leather couch. The rest of them—her sisters, her aunts, and her sister-in-law—sat in a circle and bawled. Her younger sister had been their mother's helper, until four months ago, when she had moved into the student dorms in Jerusalem. Getting up to put the kettle on, Randa exchanged a knowing glance with Jumana, who pushed a box of tissues closer to their mother.

It was completely dark outside, and Jumana wanted to go home, suddenly craving solace with a surprising intensity. She needed Tamara. She needed to talk to her, to hold her. For a brief moment, she thought she'd wait for her mother to fall asleep and then head out quietly, returning in the morning before anyone noticed she had gone. But it wouldn't have worked. They'd wake up at dawn, and she'd never make it back by then.

She felt out of place between her mother and her married sisters and their kids. Outside, the husbands were smoking and speculating about the next day's turnout, who'd come to pay his respects, and who'd stay home. Jumana longed for these three days to be over, already. She wanted to be alone in Umm al-Fahm, though that was impossible. Where would she even sleep—with Randa in their childhood room?

She climbed the stairs to the second floor to look at the room. There was nothing of hers left in that room. The four of them—bound together by shared pajamas, socks, bras, lipstick, and eye-shadow—used to stay up talking all night. Other than herself, her youngest sister Randa was the only one still single.

Jumana checked her phone. Tamara had texted her. The screen lit up with thoughtful and intimate messages. Tamara knew her family, their traditions. She understood what Jumana was going through and had supported her decision to cut off her father. Ofri's texts seemed alien, distant in comparison. She had never been to Umm al-Fahm. She had never met the family.

JUMANA'S RELATIONSHIP WITH OFRI HAD FORMED SLOWLY, starting as a simple flirtation between colleagues who really knew nothing about each other but who, little by little, learned everything there was to know, before they even held hands. The boundaries were clear. Everyone in the hospital knew Tamara, and Jumana never took off her engagement ring outside the operating room. Had she not had that breakdown during the Gaza War, nothing might have happened with Ofri.

It was toward the end of the war, and Jumana was worn down by sleeplessness, by the constant influx of casualties, of amputees. Every once in a while, an ambulance would bring an entire family, all of them critically wounded. Death swelled around her with its smell, the smell of dried blood and soot and melted metal. She couldn't shut it out. Jumana had staggered from patient to patient —they were on emergency protocol, and the shifts were endless— trying not to look any of them in the eye.

She had refused to follow the news, blocking the flow of information. Then, one day, she and Ofri were standing by the nurses' counter after a long, awful shift—she'd had to down a shot of espresso after every patient just to keep awake—and the overhead TV was blaring the news. All Jumana wanted was to go home and sleep. Even with the caffeine coursing through her veins, she could barely stand.

Ofri was motionless, fixated. Her brother was in the armored corps, and she didn't know whether he was inside Gaza or just on the outskirts. Jumana tried not to watch, not to listen, but she couldn't help but hear. Slowly, her eyes gravitated toward the screen. She was glued to the news, never-ending, stretching through time and beyond, more real than hours, minutes, and seconds. The news stories were more real than the world itself.

Live on television, a Gaza physician, Dr. Abu al-Aiysh, was crying for help just moments after his daughters were killed. Jumana couldn't bear it and fled before her tears could flow. Ofri left with her, squeezing into the same elevator. Down in the lobby, she could have said goodbye and gone home. Instead, Ofri hugged her—or, more exactly, she caught Jumana just before she collapsed onto the floor. Ofri walked Jumana out of the building, supporting her, and Jumana, who had held back her tears through the crowded lobby, finally broke down when they reached a bench outside.

"I've met him a few times," Jumana said, crumpling a wad of tissue paper between her fingers and shoving it into her pocket, her face puffy.

Ofri didn't say anything, but her hand felt its way into Jumana's sleeve, and their fingers intertwined.

"He came to a few conferences. An amazing man. Charismatic."

She stopped. It seemed there was nothing left to say, and in any case, she didn't know if words could describe what she felt. They talked about lighter things then, though their fingers were still entangled inside Jumana's long, ungainly sleeve. Afterwards, the boundaries blurred, and the new affair overpowered Jumana's life, her world. But being in Umm al-Fahm now, it became clear to her precisely which world that was—her Tel Aviv world, the bubble she had fashioned for herself there.

Jumana went back downstairs and into the living room, packed with women. Her mother, a sack of sad wrinkles and tears, was ensconced in the large sofa. They would have to help her pull herself together and get her ready for what came next, her life without him.

After everyone had gone to bed, she and Randa whispered to each other in their old room. Randa thought of sticking it out until the end of the month, but Jumana talked her out of it. Randa was starting university, and she needed to focus on her studies, to push herself. Coming home on weekends was more than enough. They lay quietly in their beds for a while, and then Jumana said that she had to make some calls. Tamara would be waiting by the phone. She tip-toed along the hallway and downstairs to Samir's old room. Her mother's heavy breathing resounded through the open bedroom door.

Even though they talked logistics, intense feeling filtered through their words. Filled with misgivings, Jumana clung to the phone, her fingers clammy and tight. What was she thinking, letting things happen with Ofri? She and Tamara talked for a long time, until Jumana could barely keep her eyes open. An image flashed through her mind—their bed, the scent of Tamara's shampoo, the touch of her skin under the covers, her body perfectly coiled around Jumana's in their unique coalescence. It had been eight deep, intimate, wonderful years.

After they said goodnight, Jumana stopped herself from calling Ofri. She would not bind herself closer to her. Nightly phone-calls would not be part of their routine. They weren't a couple. Not yet, not ever.

But when the morning came, the night's promises melted away. Ofri arrived and gave Jumana a hug, holding her longer than the others on the hospital delegation. She sat next to her, and when Jumana rose to make more coffee, Ofri followed her to the kitchen. Held in her gaze, Jumana became flustered, tongue-tied. Upon their arrival, Ofri and the others had been hovering outside with the men, unsure what to do, standing out in their Jewishness, until someone came to inquire what they were doing there. Jumana's fourth cousin Dalal was sent to fetch her, and though her gaze immediately caught Ofri's, she still stepped out the door and thanked everybody else first for coming. Someone brought in more chairs, so that the Jewish men and women could sit unsegregated in their circle, a second one that engulfed the rest of the narrow street.

Now, as Jumana moved to fetch more coffee and cookies for her colleagues, Ofri followed her. They were finally alone, in the kitchen, standing so close that their lips nearly touched. Still, there was a constant procession in and out of the kitchen, as the women mingled in the living room.

"We can't really talk here," Jumana said to Ofri, squeezing her hand but gazing off toward the kitchen door. A strange feeling swamped her. It wasn't the feeling of the affair being discovered. It was the feeling of being closeted again, after so many years.

"It's okay. I understand," Ofri said, squeezing her hand back and then letting go. "I just wanted to check on you. Are you okay?" she said, looking into Jumana's eyes.

"I am okay. I just need these next two days to pass quietly here, and then I will be back home and see you at work." She handed Ofri two plates filled with cookies. They nodded to each other and left the kitchen.

The sun was bright, and it was getting hot in the circle that was improvised on the street, not under the shade trees. A few minutes later, her colleagues left.

They stood up, kissed Jumana goodbye, and piled into their two cars. Ofri behaved naturally, like any one of them, like there was no special connection. The two cars turned and followed the narrow streets out of Umm al-Fahm. The vacant circle was then dismantled, the chairs used to augment the men's circle. The sun was scorching. Anything not shaded was burning hot, but Jumana stood, unmindful of the heat that made her sweat, waving goodbye at the cars shrinking into the distance toward the highway. Then, she went back inside and sat back down beside her mother, sinking deeply into the leather couch.

HOURS LATER, JUMANA LOOKED OUT through the big living room windows. Everything was in a haze. The sky was a foggy blue, perforating the black shades. The sun, its indifferent games now over, was murkily setting. She still had two days left. She had greeted so many people that she couldn't remember who was who anymore, but Tamara was on her way, and so were Jumana's laptop, skin-care creams, deodorant, and clothes.

Out of the corner of her eye, she watched for Tamara's Peugeot through the big living room window. She tried not to look conspicuous. She wanted to be wholly present for her family. There was no telling when a gathering like this would happen again. She was surprised by how her nephews had grown, and she was proud of her sister-in-law, the way she put Samir in his place—the only one who dared to. Jumana glanced over at her mother to make sure she had enough to eat and drink. She wanted to stay and hold Nasreen's hand, to linger in her scent, the familiar scent of home, the scent of the Umm al-Fahm air that she had nearly forgotten. She glanced through the window again toward the street corner, at Randa, and then back at her mother. Then, she heard the distinctive clanking.

The aging Peugeot had been rattling like this for years, but she and Tamara didn't want a new one. The car was precious to them. They drove everywhere with it and did everything inside it. The Peugeot appeared, maneuvering between the chairs on the corner, looking for a parking spot.

Heart swelling and eyes tearing up, Jumana wound her way through the men and the chairs and threw herself at Tamara. She was the only person with whom she could let herself go, without embarrassment, without concealment, and with abandon. Tamara swept her up into her arms, stroked her and whispered to her to calm her down. She handed Jumana a small, densely-packed bag, and they turned to face the others.

Tamara looked into Samir's eyes, but he turned away, as if naturally. They walked into the house, where Tamara went directly to embrace Jumana's mother. Somebody stood, so that Jumana and Tamara could sit together. Her father was only just gone now, but already things had started to change.

Jumana took the bag upstairs and dropped the toiletries in the bathroom. She plugged her laptop in but fought the urge to check her emails. She looked through what Tamara had brought from Tel Aviv, in case she needed anything else from the store, before it closed.

Down in the living room, her mother was holding Tamara's hand and smiling faintly. Randa grinned at Jumana. As soon as all of the guests went home, the five of them could sit together in the living room. Maybe her mother's smile would linger.

Later that night, all of the guests disappeared, but Tamara remained. Dust from the unpaved roads swirled around the orphaned chairs and beneath the cars rolling out of the driveway. Her mother hadn't eaten, and Jumana begged her to have a piece of fruit or at least to drink some tea. Her mother's eyes, welling up with sorrow, wandered from the framed photos on the walls to his things, boldly present in the living room and kitchen. Randa brewed another pot of tea, and, after they had finished their cups, it was time to get their mother to bed. Her step was uncertain. The new solitude exhausted her. Nahel and Randa helped her up the stairs, leaving Tamara and Jumana briefly alone.

"When will you come home?" Tamara asked.

Jumana couldn't say. Her mother needed a few days to adjust to the new reality, and Jumana had the week off from work.

"I think I need to stay with her just a little bit longer," she said, as she walked Tamara to the Peugeot. Jumana's urge to get into the car and go home was tied with her desire to stay behind. Not caring whether or not anyone saw, she hugged and kissed Tamara, holding her there for a long while, until Tamara finally got into her car. Jumana watched, as the Peugeot rattled away into the distance.

Back in the bedroom, Randa was reading articles for university on her computer. Jumana flipped her laptop open too, both of them looking up every few minutes to wonder aloud what things would be like in the house from now on. Finally tired of working, they lay down and compared notes about the day, the neighborhood, and the house. They didn't mention their mother—Neither of them knew what would become of her. Jumana didn't mention that she had decided to stay. In the morning, when the *azza* was over, Randa and Nahel saw that Jumana was still there, but they didn't ask questions.

She settled into a routine. One day followed another, but still Tamara didn't press her to say when she was coming back. She expressed only sympathy. Ofri didn't ask, either. She had no idea what was going on inside of Jumana. She didn't connect the dots.

Slowly, Jumana's childhood bedroom transformed into the tidy abode of an adult. She pushed the two single beds together and moved a small desk she'd found in the basement up to the room. Everything was returning to normal, again. Her mother was back in the kitchen, and the grandchildren were running around the house. But Jumana was still there.

She couldn't explain herself, not to her family, not to Tamara, not to her work. She attached herself to her mother, to Nahel, to the food, to the long-lost feeling of home. Her father's death had breathed new life into the house for her.

Naturally, her mother was happy to have her, but in time Tamara began to worry. Her anxieties increased with each passing day. It had been nearly two weeks now, and she couldn't understand how they had become so distant, with Jumana on this impromptu vacation. Still, Jumana stayed on.

When she wasn't at home, Jumana walked around town, climbing up and down the hills. She had become part of the neighborhood, stopping to chat with familiar-looking passersby whose faces she had nearly forgotten. They, too, were getting reacquainted with her.

She wandered the roads and alleyways that she had run down screaming and squealing with her friends, as a child. She walked past her kindergarten teacher's house, past her grade-school. After graduation, she had been banished from the neighborhood to a remote, private high-school. Now, she was re-christening Umm al-Fahm. The space and the view were hers to seize. She was a part of it. Suddenly, she belonged, again.

One pre-agreed return date passed and then another. Jumana ran out of vacation days from work. She visited Tel Aviv for a few nights, and Tamara said to her, patiently, "Come back already. I don't understand what is going on."

Jumana tried to explain, insisting that her mother needed somebody there. Randa and Nahel had gone back to university, she said, but Tamara looked at her in disbelief. "It does not mean that you have to throw your life away to be with your mother," she said, her voice cracking. "Samir is just next door, and your nieces and nephews are there all the time."

"I just need more time. Please give me some more time," Jumana begged, and left again, when the weekend was over, promising nothing.

One day, a family friend, an anesthesiologist who had stopped in to pay his condolences a few days earlier, called to say that they were short on doctors at his hospital. Maybe, she could drop by?

Jumana was intrigued. Maybe, she'd come, she said, just to take a look, just to see what the facilities were like and if she liked the staff. Maybe, this would be the way to forget about Ofri, completely. They had barely spoken, since her visit. There was a time when a week without Ofri would have been unimaginable, but now, here, in Umm al-Fahm, life was so much easier.

On the way to the hospital, Jumana pulled over at a store to buy more sheets, towels, and odds-and-ends for her room, for the house. She hadn't told Tamara about the job opportunity. She had fallen into the habit of hiding things from her. Calling Tamara these days felt like checking in with someone abroad. Her sisters, brothers, sisters-in-law, and all their kids and babies came by every day. Her Tel Aviv habits and routines had disappeared without a trace.

Still, she was undecided, and it was through indecision that she took the job. She became even more deeply entrenched in her old neighborhood.

Tel Aviv was far away, beyond hills and mountains, rivers and traffic jams, and another week passed, before Jumana finally drove back. She and Tamara talked, but no decisions were made. None— There wasn't anything she could say, really, because Tamara didn't have the full picture. Tel Aviv oppressed Jumana with its heat and the thick, sticky humidity. Her body craved the dry, northern air. Whenever she was with Tamara in their home, her mind wandered back to the childhood home that she had reclaimed.

Tamara came to visit every once in a while. She even stayed overnight, but eventually, the exhausting drives and the uncertainty wore her down. Jumana's retorts to her questions were impatient and unsatisfying, and she herself was distant now, as distant as Ofri was.

Jumana thought, I took this new job for her, too. I took this new job for Tamara. But how could she tell her that, considering the truth that they were drawing further and further apart? She and Tamara barely spoke, anymore. Their phone-calls were short and riddled with silences. Jumana had stopped suffering from the itch of betrayal.

Umm al-Fahm enveloped her. The town had never been hers before the way it was, now. Each evening, she and her mother would cook dinner and then settle in front of the television. Every once in a while, they would drive up north to visit Jumana's aunt, and Randa visited every weekend. Jumana and her mother picked her up from the bus-stop. On the ride home, the three of them would talk everything over.

Even her mother, now free of him, her deceased husband, participated. She and Jumana drew closer every day, as she did with Nahel and Randa.

Sometimes, Jumana thought of what it would be like if Tamara were there. She wanted her to move, to immigrate, to live with her here in this town, but she couldn't ask her to do that. It was unthinkable. It made absolutely no sense, no more than a sad joke.

The end was becoming more and more real, as real as her new job, as real as the road that she took every day from Umm al-Fahm to the new hospital and back again. She drove up at sunrise and down at sunset. How long and exhausting the drive to Tel Aviv was in comparison.

The three days a week she had allotted to Tamara were wearisome, joyless. They didn't feel like a vacation. No, they were melancholic, and they dragged.

Whenever she had to head out to Tel Aviv, Jumana drove slowly, her foot barely pressing the gas pedal. She counted the miles. She and Tamara fought constantly. She knew that they couldn't go on like this. Jumana was relieved every Sunday, when she got into the car to return home to Umm al-Fahm. Her mind wandered up into the sky, out over the sea, off through the sunset, refusing to set on the future, sinking into the past, into the present, into the near and the known. There was nothing left to say.

Saman Zoleikhaei

A FEW MEMORIES IN A WALL-LESS ROOM

Each and every night
when I seek 'round for my lost head,
darkness comes to lop it off again
in the alleyway of an unpeopled town;
the shadow of a finger-less hand
bangs me there like a hammer on a nail;
the feet of the town's lords
make their ways—like knives—
into the very pupils of my eyes
and there then pass through the land of my wound.

Today they carried back from the graveyard
a living corpse which had died a long time ago.
They said: He knows no one and is known by no one;
so it has been told that he will die, thereupon
unveiling the mysteries of the grave.

The town grew restless.
The fire of fear an' shock raged in the whole heart parts of its people. But I am not shock-struck at all 'cause I was living some while ago with a comrade of mine in a rust-covered and sorrow-ridden room.

Whilst today no one knows,
his corpse wipes away the sweat
from weary rivers' brows.

His dreams have been thrown away
in the thirsty desert sands.

I ran away in a hurry.
My comrade isn't around, I am sure;
I wish—Gracious God—
to be my father
having come to life once more,
I said.

Hey dear daddy,
the rain shower of long an' love
to meet one more mere time
disturbs my sleep
and plants the thorn of torture
in the terrain of my body.
Hey dear daddy,
it's been years now
that I'm wandering around
looking for your grave-bereft corpse;
when to wash away from my shadow your ghost?

Hey my sorrowful wife,
here and now,
far from your dark eyes,
far from your sparkling eyes,
far from my father,
far from my captured comrade,
in a wall-less room,
I'll melt away there in

the waiting foams that froth from
the mouth of a wearied rider-less horse.
Hey my black-eyed lady,
I do call you; but my throat
hangs sound on the gibbet.
I shall not say that the minaret
turned into a gravestone of this town.
I shall not say that I love you.
I shall not ask
where my captured comrade is.
Oh, my sorrowful lady.

I love you.
I do love you.
Long live my killed comrade.

At the daybreak of 15 November 1969, when I was given the news of my own death, I cried a while for my brief life. I made my way to the arms of a rain-less cloud. The cloud raised a goblet of whiskey and said: I can take you to no islet, where death fails to reach.

I said: How shall I be sure that you are not drunk?
The cloud said: On one condition.

I ran away before hearing the reply in full.

I stashed my riders' lances away in the pupils of my eyes. I tied a black cloth ('cause of my death) 'round my forehead and threw myself into the reft roads.

The roads fail to bear an' brace love.
The roads are adorned with whorehouses.
(Are they likely throwing a party for my death?)
This question stole
a couple of tear drops
from my blurred eyes.
The whores encircled me:
—Hey fellow, do not go away.
—Catch him. It is he, himself.
—Catch him.
I did burst into tears once more;
this time, however, for the whores.

As the homeless and the hungered of this town
put their hands into those of the wind,
with their graves in their own very hands,
step there-over our dead corpses,
step there-over our numbed corpses
all toward the other side of the walls;
and the mouth of the wound
in the heart of reft mountains
opens to welcome a headed-in-a-huff caravan,
my lost head led by the sun's sighs
comes back to the room of my body.
My killed comrade, as well, returns.

—Baghdad 1973

Edward Bruce Bynum

TALKING WITH KUNDALINI ABOUT THE CHILDREN OF FORCE AND LIGHT

I am the I am of *aum*, and so teach me
the dark equation between death and eternity,
and I will follow you, watch you being

a spider
among butterflies and snakes,
loving them equally

as they live, fight, and eat.
I've watched you eat my own body with events and diagnostics.
You have nothing against fingernails growing in the casket,

shoelaces of the newly dead
tossed behind the closet door, or enamel peeling from the ceiling
of cheap hotels.
I say this because I also know

you have dined with the children of force and light,
opened their skulls, dissolved the chandeliers,
swept away the cauls of time and memory
in the green and liquid world

men wrap themselves in. They go hand in hand
when the rain is talking, move like thigh into thigh.
Did you hide inside that animal's voice?

When I was a child a horse named Mister Ed
talked to me through my television set
about hidden things in people's hearts.
No one else could hear.
That was the first joke about transmigration I got,

that everything was conscious,
every cell of venous blood,
running low on oxygen,
was swimming its way back upstream to the lungs and heart.
You are a sexual science,

an ambitious tree. When I
cross my arms and lie down in the grass,
a hundred billion primates
walk back through time toward me.

The weirdest thing is when I dream.
Sometimes, the screen flows,
a hole opens in the middle,
a spike of light drills up into my brain from a dark watery place,

tossing out shadows,
scaring all the chickens to hell.
Like a thick mammal,

its eye rides in the light up a vehement elevator,
then off the top, off the balconies, the rooftops,
the roads, and data banks illegal to men.

Birds fly with the children of force and light.
I know because
a doctrine in the wind catalogues this.
In a remote sanctuary,

after a thousand years of dreaming, monks
awaken into this. There is water not totally of the earth.
One day, after leaving the birch trees, the almonds, the sea,

I'll fold a cube of darkness around myself in a great arc.
I'll pull in the echo of my own light.
I'll carry the branch back.

You are the starfish on the beach who whispers 'fuck me,'
the alien abduction that makes perfect sense.
Every time I read poetry,

ghosts appear through you. Vermeer's colors
inflame the trees, shadow the ground
with white, green, and bronze,

like light spinning around inside the pearl of an earring.
A great calla lily stands in the dark. There is an ocean
pretending to be your body

I can only talk to from a distance,
throw flat stones skimming across its surface
in waves and salt.

Today is not a good day for drowning.
I know that. I know we are always swimming, flying,
flowing to you and back out and through you again,

shiny fish in the sluice gates of the night sky, full of small fires
you can see from the pier. They live in their own galaxy
beyond algae,
have their own religion,

wonder if anything conscious dwells beyond their shore.
It is the same with a friend of mine
who last week took full ownership of his cancer. He

realized they were partners
through many lifetimes,
opening the doors for each other, going to weddings,

watching their hair grow thinner,
the kitchen lights flickering on and off,
with the ventriloquist in the bathroom
making bad jokes.

Ancient men had a song about that horse
who dreamed himself into a man on our watch.
His voice did not change.

His eyes remained huge, separated by a great nose and space
allowing him to think,
gather memories into his brow like winter berries
stored in a jar for a cold night

when witches are riding the tree branches, when it's raining,
and the darkest of birds restrain themselves
from even stray thoughts. Because of this,

or simply because my own hair is thinning,
I recall a summer day when a stink bug flew by me twice
on the back deck,

then later that night seeing a black galleon in the sky
with its cruel moon, its captain hauling slaves.
The lime on his tongue

helped keep the keel of the ship afloat throughout my sleep.
The rum was arbitrary.
I pulled him up from the sea,
from legends in the waters,

from hypnotic ingredients found only
when we are falling backward through space,
and there is no room for mediation or leaves or stones.

What if an octopus used its arms
to gather the sorrows of time together? Would it be enough
if suddenly the wind identified itself by name;

Would you still hear millions of voices repeating in syncopation
"I love you"? If the sun and moon went off together,
never returning to this dimension, would you still see the soul,

and its doppelganger, the pineal gland in the middle of the skull,
open like a black hole available for travel when entered,
the waves of space around you bending,

you in control of the senses
of sight, smell, hearing, taste, and touch?
You are the first cannibal of real beauty to speak to me.

You are Isis with pants down, no regrets.
You, an apple orchard suddenly full of peaches,
confuse a dreaming farmer.

You are weather in the distance,
creating the future. You, the spores on a frog,
changing the microbes, warning of tomorrow.

Yes, I have idled asleep in the engine of my soul,
while you taught the secret logic of gravity. Because love
breathes in you, not the body,

I know you and love and I are immortal,
apostasy in this age of chewing gum and glass.
I dreamed I made a green voyage once.

You were there. The trees were green, the leaves were green,
the backwaters of the sea were green,
the houses on the hill overlooking them, all were green.

I thought even the voices of the gulls were green,
so that they could call the mussels below the shoreline
to open and close without fear;

that the seaweed's faith was green, piles of salt collecting
under the kelp had a name
called by the waves; I thought if I could push my fingers
deep enough into the sand

I would feel the heartbeat of thousands swimming here,
astonished and weary to a new continent.
I write poetry secretly like sex.

I am the clown in the cemetery weeping for his dog.
You are as common as money,
wet as adultery.

A blue flag flies over you.
I know because the hours have eyes,
because hope is a bottle floating,

because following you is to be alive, with metal,
with spiders, with trumpet swans carrying me home,
because when Odysseus died, he traveled far enough south

in time to become a black man. So, when the dead
follow you through the canal of the last breath, reach
the white fish of light in the distance, they are always amazed

at how much they already know or start remembering again,
when the rivers above the head flow
down into the great teaching science.
I doubt there are Mondays and Tuesdays

among the remote stars we travel to
between deaths. I doubt entry into this world
is not without error and clumsy administration.

A mule knows this as much as a snake, both
dimly aware of the distinct vibration
they share with the outer constellations.
It is folk knowledge among the oysters,

a ballet you have choreographed, a resonant gospel
heard when buying peas and onions at market,
when your ears are wide open to the songs of the Cheyenne

or conversations of the fireflies. I recall
a great moth coming toward me once, a little like
that white fish, only thinner, with a pulse

somewhere between smoke and the exertion of an eel.
Plenty of others have lost the trail of you,
becoming mendicants, shoe fitters, bankers,

lending their own mothers out under the cold hide of the moon
in exchange for a portfolio and a knife.
I wear two watches, one for this world,

one for the next. I have appointments
that must be kept, souls growing around me I've come to know,
who make me wiser, thicker, more lenient

than the wind. Yes, I find you under the wheelbarrows
I rode as a child, in the persistent mystery of grass.
The only way

to find mercy in a diamond
is to pierce through the heart of the Buddha.
At least that's what the orchids say.

O my Beloved, who would have believed
twenty-five hundred years after Gautama,
two millennia after Christ,

fourteen centuries from the passing of the prophet,
you would reappear in me, awake, conscious,
sinusoidal rhythm of every religion,

surge point in the Homo sapien heart. Blood understands,
feels the stones shift. An elegant linguist
lives in the upward coil of tobacco pipe smoke.
Consciousness on these outer planes is just matter
and stuff, you know.

Deeper currents are in the tides
through all that is, was, or can be,
for which there is no mental description.

It is weeping in an orchard
full of ravenous birds who know you write music,
follow the orbit of mysterious stars,

many of whom are cannibals swollen with dark matter;
it is dying your hair completely white, then
visiting the gallows,

hoping to meet someone
on the holy days of the month. It is
the tale of the two fishermen and the gambler

who set sail on the sea
and arrive at the homeport of the vampire they love.
All crystals in the pineal gland

align; there is a blue flash of radiance.
A serpent arrives
barreling through like a train escaped from the Andes.

It is heading up the coast where the sand is perpetually clear,
seagulls in the air, weightless beings,
watching for millions of years.

Joseph Thomas

THE NOT-SO-LEARNED ASTRONOMER

Words tattooed over muscles
wander-wrap down to thick wrists.
At 6 ft 7 in, he stands closer than I
to the heavy gauge wire mesh
bolted atop 20 ft cement walls
lit by supernatural halogen
above the dirty basketball court
we call the "outside."

His eyes wander past our confines
to the only twinkling speck
in our polluted scrap of winter sky.
He asks, "Professor…
You are a professor, right?
Tell me,"—as he
points to a distant spot of light—
"is that a planet or a star?"

And I, whose doctorate in literature
neither makes me professor
nor learned astronomer,
explain assuredly that it is probably Venus,
given its angle to the horizon, its magnitude.
I even say, "You can be sure
if it has a faint green sheen."
But I don't know any of that, really.

My fellow inmate's eyes squint.
His face scrunches. He searches
through the haze for that special green,
then glumly says, "I can't tell.
It's too hard to see," and walks away.
It's no surprise. I am sure
that in this light, from this place
no one can be sure
if it's a planet or a star.

Your Vessel | Sarah Walko

Kwong Kwok Wai
Rachel Ng, Translator

BLUE-AND-WHITE PORCELAIN BOWL

MAAN, ONE

TO CONSTRUCT, BOWL BY BOWL, a city of one's mind can take a lifetime. Recalling Ah Yau's words at the *dai pai dong*, I watched images of blue-and-white florals with their understated cerulean hue slowly begin to surface in the bowl, as I spooned up the *congee*. My mind had been porcelain-white and void of thought. Painted in strokes alternately realistic and abstract, the florals of the bowl depicted a metaphysical world.

I remembered such blue-and-white bowls—simple and elegant, familiar yet distant. I didn't know how many years it had been since I'd last used this kind of bowl.

The blue-and-white florals I remembered were jagged, irregular—What must have held the brush wouldn't have been a hand but a tousled, determined mind, bursting to say something, to say it quickly, to paint it out before the thought slipped away, to record a time long-gone and the kind of life gone with it.

A flower must have blown in from the window, a flower that was alive, one that could decay, a real flower of intense fragrance. But wait, it couldn't be real. No bloom could really be that fragrant, so fragrant that it made the day seem vibrant and beautiful, the scent not unlike the feeling of falling head over heels in love.

I finished my meal, tied my long hair back in a ponytail, put on my knapsack, and headed down the road to the distant hill.

What of the so-called flower—Did I leave it at the *dai pai dong*? Or was I just overthinking things? There were no flowers along the way, but the intoxicating smell permeated the air. My knapsack was filled with his things: soap, a change of clothes. It was breaking my back, as I hiked up the hill.

I had also packed a small floral-patterned bowl. Maybe, the bumpy hike had shattered it and somehow released the floral scent.

I reached into my knapsack and pulled out a triangular piece of broken ceramic. The shard fit perfectly between my thumb and index finger. Only half of the blue-glazed flower was visible on this fragment, but its bud was intact. The flat piece was wedged between my two digits, as though webbing had grown. I brought it closer to my nose, sniffed it carefully, and sniffed again.

Yau, One

The only audible sounds were a series of clinks, like porcelain pieces knocking against each other. Siu Maan used to say that she came often to this part of the hill, when she was a child. The water mortars here didn't look like water mortars; there were only holes of sand. If she hadn't repeatedly told me so, I would not have believed that this could once have been a watermill. Squatting down on the slope and staring aimlessly at this mountainous waste land, I had not a single thought in mind, yet I was unable to find peace. I'd left a message for the National Party last month. They'd never responded, not even with a brief message. Now, I didn't know whether or not to hope for a response.

Should I hike up further? Would I find more space and a better view? I would be able to see the lights at the edge of the city from afar, as well as the great railroads and highways stretching into the city centre. On the other side of the river would be the Mainland, with its even more extensive networks and infrastructure.

No, I'd rather seek cover from the trees and bushes and let the city lights be shrouded by the darkness. I heard an indistinct rumbling noise, perhaps a few musical notes from memory, rather than the true rumble of a train engine. There shouldn't have been a whisper of sound in an abandoned wilderness such as this.

Still, I needed to enter into that realm of strong, spirited percussion, that realm of symbols. I needed to leap up and ride on a musical note in flight, to escape the phenomenal world around me. The city kept calling me, calling me, imploring me to make change.

I ran down the hill from the watermill, diving deep into the ominous darkness of the woods. Each step was taken with great force, so as to shatter completely the shards of ceramic tiles I carried in the knapsack; with great force, so as to eliminate all traces of sound. No, I did not want to hear even a whisper of sound.

In the darkness, there appeared to be a spot of blue on one tree, while another one seemed tinged with red. As I walked deeper into the woods, the trees turned even more scarlet. This was no *trompe l'oeil* but an unveiling of the phenomenal world, an uncovering of the truth within me. I heard an indistinct sound of winding clockwork, a fascinating shade much like the reddish tinge beneath flesh and skin.

Then, I heard the sound of footsteps. I turned quickly. It was Ah Yau, panting and out of breath, leaning against the cow mill fence, with a knapsack on his shoulders.

Maan, Two

There was a narrow gap in the wire fence that only allowed the passage of one person. I'd lived here for many years as a child, and

I'd never noticed it. Yet Ah Yau had discovered it upon his first visit—as though I'd been blind.

In fact, I didn't have much memory of this village. What had left the deepest impression upon my mind was hiking up the hill to scavenge for bowls. Back then, there hadn't yet been any fencing, and the entire piece of land was covered with bowls, just lying around. In my naiveté, I thought the hill so magical as to grow ceramic pieces from the earth. On the other hand, my parents regarded the whole thing as a matter of course.

Only many years later, when I left the village, did I realize that this was once a place for making ceramic pottery, home to a kiln that had been built during the Ming and Qing dynasties. Historical facts aside, however, I could only remember that bowl—the little rice bowl that wasn't shabby, though not pretty either. Some things one only appreciates after their loss. I didn't need Ah Yau to remind me of this truth. That day, when I first brought him here to tell him my story of these broken pieces, he was unexpectedly enthused, nattering on about treasure-hunting.

Long-limbed and insect-thin, Ah Yau tilted slightly to the left and eased half his body through the gap. Where there used to be bowls and plates were now scattered broken pieces. Occasionally, a hand-painted flower on a white crane's wing was still discernible, along with other florals and a long-tailed bird.

"We used these kinds of bowls at the *dai pai dong* back when we were children," Ah Yau exclaimed, as he gathered his hoard. He examined each piece closely, venturing deeper and deeper to the foot of the hill, as if he were leading some excavation mission.

The piece of land circled by the fence was without grass. The ground looked especially dark at night, like a bottomless pit. Ah Yau stretched his arm out full length to pluck up two porcelain pieces with some fish or chrysanthemum pattern, while bending at an awkward angle to avoid the other broken shards. His pose looked dangerous, as though he were about to fall into the abyss.

I wanted to reach out and grab his hip, his belt, or something—but my better sense of judgement told me that this was nothing but a piece of muddy land. He could fall and land, anywhere. I did not need to be afraid.

I edged toward him nonetheless, not daring to hold him. All the senses in my body were alert—If the slightest mishap were to occur, I would set aside all hesitation and come to his rescue.

Clink-clink-clink. For a moment, I couldn't tell whether the sound was that of ceramic pieces, of teeth clacking, or simply of someone's too-boisterous laughter.

Ah Yau handed over a fragment with half a chrysanthemum bloom. Elegantly curved, it was broken from the well of a bowl.

Afraid that it would cut my hand, I gingerly held the shard between my fingers, flipping it back and forth. Its arcing shape looked like a sail stretching in the breeze, borne on the wind. The angle of the arc was so slight, so gentle. This thought, in turn, seemed to make the piece weightier in my hand. I began to feel less concerned about cutting my hand, and instead turned the shard over repeatedly, observing it from different angles and positions. It wasn't quite crescent-shaped, for it was a bit too round, though I wouldn't call it a hemisphere either, with its gracefully curved edge. The more I looked at it, the more it seemed like a real, scented flower petal.

Ah Yau found another piece but smugly refused to show it to me. In retaliation, I clutched my piece firmly in my fist, hiding it from him.

"Watch out it doesn't cut your hand," he said.

I responded with a smirk.

The curve of the piece was perfectly in sync with the shape of my palm, as though they were made for each other.

"I never knew that this was meant to be a crane," Ah Yau said, as he observed the piece in his hand, his voice tinged with nostalgia. "I would look at these bowls whenever I ate *congee*, and never once managed to guess what the pattern was supposed to be."

"I thought they were just meaningless doodles," I said, though I was certain that his piece was a crane.

"I think I can draw better than this."

More broken laughter.

Our hands hid razor-sharp fragments of broken ceramic. We agreed to wear them around our necks. Back then, everything we said seemed to be just empty words—Who could take such silly banter seriously?

Yau, Two

There was an abandoned public school in the village. At first I wanted to sleep there, but the wood lice made this impossible. It was better to sleep on the hill, where the water mill was. The mill was covered with sand—coarse and rough, a dark shade of burnt yellow. I dug my shoes deep into the sand, hoping that this would polish the filth off of my soles.

I turned and burrowed my whole body into the sand, worming my way in, over and over again. What compelled me to do this? A sweat broke out, and an uncomfortable wave of heat moved through me. I slammed my body against the sand, and tiny pricks of pain exploded over me like fireworks.

A muffled echo reverberated through the quiet day. Then, I

started wriggling again, desperate to rub off all the filth on my clothes, on my body.

Corrosion is a process of purification. Like the rusting of metal, the piece-by-piece erosion of the phenomenal world, the wearing away of confusion and insecurity.

I remembered a T-shaped street. At the end of the street was our *dai pai dong*, just around the corner from the footbridge. A plastic canvas hung between the bottom of the bridge and the shop.

I had no opinions as to what dishes to offer our customers or what kinds of noodles to serve. My sole request was to use blue-and-white porcelain bowls—That was it, take it or leave it. None of my partners had objections, so we asked Siu Maan to hurry and try to sort things out. When the first batch of bowls arrived at the stall, we unwrapped them from the paper packages, washed them, and used them to serve deep-fried bread sticks and sweet soup on the wooden tables. It was as though my past childhood had returned right before my eyes.

When I was small, Mum used to love buying leftover deep-fried bread sticks after picking me up from school, because they were so cheap. To make sweet soup, she'd soak the bread sticks in a large blue-and-white soup bowl with crane patterns. Afterward, she'd divvy up the soup into smaller bowls, some of which were adorned with leafy patterns. Others were dotted with peach-red blossoms and had the words "Boundless Longevity" painted at the base.

Every Sunday, our *dai pai dong* sold old, second-hand things. People from the neighborhood brought unwanted objects from home, cluttering the plastic tables and chairs by the street. Most of it was trivial junk you could take away for free. Some of the better-quality goods were sold for a couple of dollars. The junk piled up underneath the tent canvas, as if this were a refugee camp. Some of the people in the neighborhood called this a shelter from typhoons and landslides.

In our banter, someone said, "Why don't we just build an image of the past?"

Everyone laughed and then fell silent.

I looked quietly at the piles of junk on the floor—old fabric, old dresses, old textbooks—and wondered what "the past" actually meant. The past seemed to be an idea both silly and insignificant.

Maybe, it means a period of time? Or maybe, the form of a place at a given point in time? Siu Maan said that it's but a feat of imagination; because you are not satisfied with today, you imagine other things.

She was responsible for cooking *congee* on holidays. She never added scallops. Instead, she used ginkgo nuts and a small amount of tofu skin, but she boiled everything to such a mushy state that it would have been impossible to tell what the ingredients were, if she hadn't told me.

When I got up in the morning, the *congee* would be ready. Sometimes, I would scoop it out into the crane bowl or the bat bowl, but often I would just look and not take a single sip. I disliked the plain, insipid taste. When she discovered my sentiment, she added preserved fruit peels, but I scolded her for doing this.

In the warm morning sun, there were bubbles in the *congee*, a voice rising from the bowl, yet I couldn't make a coherent story of this. The bland white of the *congee* made the white bowl seem even more pale, so pale that there was nothing more to say.

Perhaps, I was hoping for a story worth telling, one with a proper beginning and end, with plot twists and a satisfying conclusion—Only then, it seemed, would there be some sort of explanation.

But what kind of sound was I looking for, really? I listened for it at the *dai pai dong* back then. I listened for it now, as I hid in the hills. I listened for it in the bowls, then in the sand.

As I pressed my ear against the sand, I seemed to hear the sounds of people working, stacking up bowls, transporting them in a ceramic kiln of former days. I heard the sounds cradled inside the bowls, all familiar sounds that I'd heard before. These were the sounds of yesterday—sounds of flurried activity, eating and drinking, shouting hawkers, dribbling basketballs, and the low muttering of queues.

Burying half my face in the sand, I felt like a big rock sinking into the sea. Would there be deathly silence there? Or a cacophony of sounds?

At the very bottom of the sandy earth lay also the confused sound of history. Yes, as Siu Maan said, it wasn't just a childhood memory but also a "history" that people speak of, ancient history of bygone days.

This was the filth left behind by history. Some say that my ideas are filth, but in my view, to forbid me from thinking such thoughts would be truly filthy. Corrosion, or the removal of such filth, is a game of shooting moving targets. In this game, I was no sniper but a target; and what moved were not the targets but the snipers. What was shot dead were parts of our own selves.

In the cracking earth grew a creeper plant with hard, cold leaves. They pricked at the back of my neck. They made me think of winter days. They seemed to clear extra space for thoughts, though nothing seemed to stick.

I felt a repeated corrosion of self, to the extent that I felt completely weightless. I felt at the back of my neck a lightness, a sting—a sting of both pain and pleasure.

Under what circumstances did destruction not count as destruction, anymore? If I had in my possession one short year—one short year in this life—would it deserve to be snuffed out in the long expanse of "history," simply because of its brevity? Must we give up the small things for the sake of the bigger picture, give up individual and subjective agency?

I remembered a video I'd watched once on the Internet, a showdown between a mantis and a rat.

If under certain pre-conditions, a result was bound to happen, can we still say that it happened without reason?

Maan, Three

A group of five of us came together to open the *dai pai dong.* Some were primary schoolmates. Some were online friends. I was the odd one out. At first the partners' wives and girlfriends tagged along, and so did I; but later, they said that spouses and family members should not join for fear of complicating things. So, Ah Yau said that I was not his girlfriend, and I came along.

The *dai pai dong* was operated in an idiosyncratic way, with a menu that made little sense. *Congee* was offered but no rice, milk tea but no coffee, instant soup noodles but no fried noodles. I asked Ah Yau about this, but he just shrugged and continued to focus on his bowl. The crane and bat bowls were used for plain *congee.* The rooster bowl was used for soup noodles with spiced pork cubes. Service was executed with military precision.

Later on Sundays, we also served lime and orange squash and 7-Up with salted lemon, as beverage options. When I asked Ah Yau why, he explained that as a child, he would go to the tea restaurant at the front of his housing estate and order lime and orange squash, while his mum ordered 7-Up with salted lemon.

I didn't come to the *dai pai dong* every Sunday. Only on holiday mornings, when I had nothing else to do and when it felt right. Things were busiest just before lunchtime. We'd run out of both crane and rooster bowls. Eventually, we'd resort to using the "Boundless Longevity" bowls.

Ah Yau would wash dishes frantically at the back of the stall. He never slacked off for the sake of his crane bowls; nor did he ever stop insisting that instant noodles were best matched to the rooster bowls. As the busiest holiday shift drew to a close before dusk, he'd finish washing, stack the bowls up high, and arrange them meticulously. At this quiet hour, he would tend to his bowls like a bartender with his glasses, using a white cloth to dry and polish each one.

"Benches. Why don't you have benches around here?" the last customer to leave before the close of day asked, empty rooster bowl in hand.

We all turned to look at each other, speechless. The customer realized that we had never seen any such "benches ," so he took a thick pack of cards from his bag and began busily flipping through the deck. The pack looked strange. Smaller than poker playing cards, the cards of this deck were long and thin, so much so that they looked like ladyfingers.

Finally, he showed us one of the cards in the deck, on which was the picture of a small bench.

"How can you have a *dai pai dong* without this?" The old man ran his hand through the few strands of silver hair on his head, smiling kindly.

Three days later, he brought us a long wooden bench and even taught us how to play with those ladyfinger cards.

The full deck was used for a game called Fifteen Wu, half the deck for Tien Gow, and a quarter of the deck for Pai Gow, each with their own set of rules.

The cards were given to us as a gift, and we placed them in a blue-and-white bowl, like flowers in a vase. The bowl was set on one end of the bench, with a light bulb dangling over it—just like a piece of installation art.

Now, at the edges of this quiet, remote village, I sat with Ah Yau, perched on a stone bench outside of the public school. The long stone-hewn bench made me think of the old wooden bench at the *dai pai dong.*

There hadn't been any news for the past few days, but Ah Yau didn't dare return home. He wanted to lay low for a few more days. As he sat chewing on a rock-hard piece of ox-tongue pastry, there was no doubt he was complaining silently that I hadn't brought *congee* to make the pastry go down a bit easier.

I could not stop thinking about the old wooden bench and refused to let go of the image. I fell into a dark tunnel of thought. That deck of ladyfinger cards told the story of the old man's world, a world that we youngsters had never known, an era well before our time. Yes, indeed, everyone was simply holding one-sided conversations, describing worlds in their own words, narrating the hows, whys, and what-must-bes on their own terms.

Yau, Three

One Sunday morning, word came that someone was forming a National Party.

"Are we a nation?"

"That goes without saying."

Siu Maan listened quietly, as the neighborhood and the regular customers gathered together in a frenzied, spirited discussion.

"We have our own collective memories that aren't shared by others, right?"

"But listen. Na-tion. It sounds so big and important."

"Fine, then what's a nation?"

It's said that every common man has a duty toward the matters of his country, but the most common conversation topic of this day was really buttered pineapple buns and radish with pig skin. The subsequent Sunday, the two dishes were added to the menu.

Meanwhile, the regulars formed a habit of coming to the *dai pai dong* every Sunday, for both the political banter and the food.

It was unclear whose idea it was, but it didn't matter where the idea came from, as long as everyone agreed with it. We gave a new name to the buttered pineapple buns. Nation Buns. As for how to convey our messages, there was a fierce but grounded debate over whether we should carve them out on each piece of butter, or just sandwich a ladyfinger card in the middle of the buns.

Anyway, at some point we would spread some kind of important message, and in secret. So, I thought.

Evenings were a quiet time for the *dai pai dong*. Siu Maan sat on one end of the wooden bench, where she played with the ladyfinger cards distractedly. To cheer her up, I showed her some research I'd found. She flipped through the pages and read out the title, "The Song of the Yue Boatman."

"It's all gibberish to me," I said.

"Yue, as in Cantonese?"

I didn't take the pages back. Instead, I motioned for her to read them through them, carefully.

I added, "It turns out that, in the past, people who lived here spoke differently from the way that we speak now."

"What do you mean by *here*?" she asked.

"Well, Yue used to be a very large region that stretched from the Lingnan area to Guangdong, Guangxi, and even to Vietnam and the north of Thailand. It was a vast stretch of land."

"Oh?"

"This was a long time ago—before the Qin dynasty. A vast kingdom."

"I've heard that some Vietnamese use this as a reason to claim that this is Vietnamese territory, that we've taken their land."

Whether there was any malice in Siu Maan's words, I could not tell, but that wasn't the point. The point was that things had changed, changed irrevocably.

We left a message for the National Party via Facebook, and as we waited and waited for their response, word arrived that they had been banned. This was news to us.

Nothing much had changed, but all of a sudden the atmosphere turned sour. The neighborhood grew nervous, and our Sunday meetings had to be canceled. Truly, nothing at all had happened, but no one in the group wanted to talk anymore; even the *dai pai dong* had to close.

Often, it only takes a single loose screw to dismantle the phenomenal world.

MAAN, FOUR

THE DEEP-FRIED BREAD STICKS I'd brought didn't seem to suit Ah Yau's taste. He took large bites but looked utterly listless. He didn't change into the pants I'd brought him in the knapsack, nor did he change his T-shirt. Although his hair, his sleeves, and his shoes were covered with sand, he didn't seem to have any intention of shaking any of it off.

Next to the abandoned school on the hill was a museum, which almost never had visitors. The guard in the front room didn't seem to care about security, so we sneaked in through the back door with some food. The museum was the only place on the hill that was air-conditioned, and I thought that we'd be more comfortable eating inside.

Ah Yau squatted next to a glass display case and chowed down half a bread stick. He ripped the remaining half into small pieces and soaked them in the *congee*. I squatted down with him, leaning against the other side of the display case, facing a small window that opened up to a view of the sky.

"I brought you an old pair of pants."

After a long silence, he said in a throaty rasp, "There's really no need." As he spoke, he jiggled the toe of his shoe from left to right, playfully toying with the sand. Porcelain fragments and sand grains. These things seemed to have a magnetic hold over him.

"Your shoes, they're broken."

Or maybe what had a magnetic hold over him were broken things. The memory of him, scavenging for ceramic pieces at the cow mill, floated before my eyes. He'd examined and studied every piece, staring at each fragment with indulgence. Perhaps, he wasn't so much looking at the pieces as he was peering beyond their jagged edges, at what was invisible and unstated.

He set down the bowl and circled the small room, without saying a word.

Grains of sand stuck were stuck to the soles of his shoes, so that each step he took made a loud crunching on the concrete, as though he were walking on the edge of a precipice. I listened to the groans and grunts the sand grains made—the protests, accusations, and curses.

Out of grievance or regret, I couldn't tell which, I cursed myself for bringing him here. If we hadn't discovered that blue-and-white bowl—that bowl from another world—none of this would have happened. There would have been no talk of the *dai pai dong*, no talk of the so-called past.

There was an oddly shaped bowl in the glass case, sitting next to a plaque that read "Chrysanthemum Bowl." The plaque explained that the piece was an inferior good, damaged in the manufacturing process and thrown out of the lot. I clasped the small porcelain fragment that Ah Yau had given me, a shard now hanging from my neck, still hidden under my shirt. I wondered if the complete chrysanthemum pattern would look the same as the one on the oddly formed bowl in the glass case.

There was also a "Plum Blossoms and Knotted Branches Bowl" chipped in two places; the remaining well of a "Bat Bowl"; and half of a "Bamboo Leaves Bowl," shaped like a water ladle. Holding the fragment tightly in my fist, I felt that it no longer seemed like a flower petal but a small spade, uncovering the topmost layer of the earth's surface. Beneath our feet, beneath the shiny floorboards of this museum, and hidden in the many layers of soil and grime, would be innumerable blue-and-white bowls.

I wondered what lay beneath the sediment, beneath this deep, peaceful stupor we were in. If it took a century to collect soil sedimentation one-inch thick, then what kind of a past could we excavate?

Ah Yau said not a word, as he walked. He was staring at the giant wall display that detailed the process of pottery-making, unconsciously grinding the sand on the soles of his shoes. There was a faraway look in his eyes. Was the world he saw a world ahead of our time? Or an ancient past, as profound as the earth itself?

The more I studied him, the less I understood him. My mind was all in a jumble. I didn't bother hiding my confusion anymore, so I blurted out, "If I hadn't brought you here in the first place to see all these bowls, I wouldn't know they meant so much to you. Maybe, everything could have been different."

The room was silent as a grave.

"Not really." He shook his head. "No, you shouldn't think that." His whole body swayed slowly back and forth, from the soles of his feet to the top of his head.

His response confused me even more, but a strange flicker of determination appeared in his eyes. He read out some of the text on the wall, describing how the pottery kiln had existed for four hundred years. These were things I'd told him before, but he kept repeating and mulling over the words, as if communicating some meaning beyond the obvious.

"Is 400 necessarily bigger than 1?" he muttered absent-mindedly. "Is four hundred seconds more significant than one? Four hundred years isn't necessarily bigger, more significant than one year, but then again, one year isn't bigger than four hundred, right?"

He stopped talking, half in pain and half-lucid. Was he silent for one second? Or for four hundred years?

Could the second that had just passed invalidate one second from yesterday? Or one second from four hundred years ago? I sensed that this was what he was gnashing his teeth over. Was there such a distinction in history between the big and the small? If a longer period of history couldn't replace a shorter one, then likewise, the more recent, intimate past couldn't invalidate an ancient history, faraway as it may seem.

YAU, FOUR

IN ANCIENT CHINA, DIFFERENT COLORS stood for the North and the South, while the East claimed the origin of all colors. The fascinating thing was that the origin of all colors was also the eternal color. This begs the question. What color was it that was both the origin and the eternal?

The color of grass, the color of hair, and the color of sky. We call them by the same name.

Or maybe, it was destined to be the color of change and volatility, ever since the dawn of time. And if it is indeed so protean by nature, maybe we can glimpse—for one short second—its true nature.

The blue-and-white florals on porcelain ceramics first appeared over a thousand years ago in the Song dynasty. Of course, what is a thousand years compared to absolute eternity?

Yet what was truly absolute?

Now, here on the hill, I believed I wanted simplicity and clarity.

I hauled my heavy, soaking self up in the pouring rain. The sand had turned muddy, and its weight was dragging me down. There was a cacophony of noises—the pitter-patter of raindrops, of rain pelting the trees; the creaking of the watermill, as though it were back in operation.

I began to arrange porcelain fragments on the sodden ground. I gathered all the pieces I could find, transported them up the hill, and laid them out one by one. I squirmed about like a worm in the middle of the clearing, spreading the fragments in all directions and leaving a small gap between pieces. Piece by piece, I assembled a blue-and-white porcelain bowl that covered the hillside. The delicate and the unrefined intermingled to form a patchy but dazzling picture, as though a brush were blurring over the edges of the pieces, stroke by stroke.

I braved the rain and ran up to the peak of the other hill, where the watermill was. I gazed down at the big porcelain dish from above. Rain water had cleansed the pieces, their cool shade of blue standing out starkly against the white.

Ah Yau must look at these flowers of muted blue—for they were a portrait of me.

Emily Murphy

ANTHROPOCENE

At the brown-shingle Casey's general store
in One-Stoplight, Illinois
seven white-haired men
forever clean-shaved
parked on faded cases of Dr. Pepper
chew the skinny ends of toothpick slivers.
"I never met her kids."
The church up on the hill has a flier
tacked over a faded orange announcement
about last winter's pheasant season,
the flier with the bird your friend drew in high school
passed through every copier in town.
"I hear she's got more in the incubator."
The circle opens for a hands-in-pockets
from out of town
holding onto a bag of over-ripe Doritos,
the ones on the floor of his truck that day,
when the corn had just broken the dirt
and his phone rang off the hook back home
waiting for the word about a person
who wasn't a person anymore.
"No, but she put that 'gator in reverse,
and she tore out of there."
The rustling of overalls like falling leaves in April,
light rain drifting down oak street
between redbrick buildings

painted with chewing tobacco signs
and black earth plots of six foot summer corn.

Emily Murphy

TECHNO-PASTORAL

& I too
lately enamored of it all
so pissed off at non-existence
I'm drawing out these words
as though by shaping
they could pass
a squirrel an elk
a Volkswagen on the roadside
like that great joke
the one that starts
a squirrel an elk
& a Volkswagen go into a bar
the joke you tell at night
when your lamp won't shut up
about the scene from Space Odyssey
where Yul Brynner
opens the monolith
gasps, "My God! It's full of fish!"
& you turn to your alarm
& promise God & all the red numbers
for the eighteenth time
you'll call this sleep thing off
in just another fifteen minutes
it's not quite dawn
& it'd be such a shame
anyway to miss the quilting together

of a new day
bus routes & spreading fog
& besides you've got to write that poem
the one that ends with the joke
that starts with a squirrel
an elk & a Volkswagen all going into a bar
& ends with a great outpouring of beer
& molasses sending up
Noah & the rest

Sandro F. Piedrahita

ALMA: VIRGIN AND MARTYR

THE SHINING PATH GUERRILLAS OCCUPIED CAJABAMBA on a Friday and, by the next Monday, the first *juicios populares*, or popular trials, had already begun. The first man to be tried was Alma's father, Rodrigo Vereau, the town's mayor. He was considered a "white man" in Peru and a "revisionist" in the eyes of the *senderistas.* As usual, all of the townspeople, including Alma and her mother, attended the "trial" under penalty of suffering the "people's punishment," if they chose not to participate.

Alma's father was tied to a tree in the center of the plaza, known as "Gloriabamba," where Alma was forced to listen to the litany of charges read against him by Lalo "Cuchillazo" Ramos, the head of the *senderistas* in Cajabamba. Cuchillazo accused Alma's father of being "anti-democratic," a "traitor against the masses," and a "capitalist dog" who had "conspired with the ruling classes to oppress the Quechua peoples and oppose the people's war." Of course, the *juicios populares* never ended in an acquittal. The conviction was pre-ordained, and so it was with Alma's father. After the charges were read, Cuchillazo asked the crowds what the punishment should be. To Alma's great surprise, the townspeople of Cajabamba, her fellow citizens, unanimously demanded that her father be killed.

"The mayor must be stoned," they cried out in unison.

A female member of the Shining Path, her face covered with a red kerchief, then handed Alma a stone, which she was supposed to throw against the mayor.

"What am I supposed to do?" she asked her mother. "I can't join in with the killing of my own father."

"Just throw it somewhere, far from his body, and nobody will ever know. That is what I intend to do. You have to do it, so that the *forasteros* do not come after us."

Then, the stoning began. The townspeople of Cajabamba, many of whom had elected her father to be their mayor, many of whom had supposedly been his friends, participated in the collective crime with relentless abandon. Some laughed. Some cheered. Some threw more than one stone and aimed at Alma's father with deadly precision. Alma felt the small, round rock in her hand. She closed her eyes, as she threw it far from her father.

"Puerco, puerco," the crowds chanted. "The mayor is a pig primed for the slaughter."

Alma turned her eyes away from her father, in order not to see how he was tortured. Still, she was close enough to the tree where her father was suffering that she could hear his cries, his exclamations of pain, at least at the beginning, until they were completely muted, and Alma knew that he was dead. She remembered when she had attended bullfights at the Plaza de Toros, averting her eyes as the matador completed *la faena* and thrust his sword through the bull's back, already bloodied by the lance of the picador.

Eventually, the *senderistas* unfastened the dead mayor from the tree and dragged him naked through the streets of Cajabamba, like a dead bull dragged by horses at the end of a bullfight. A pack of mongrel dogs every so often nipped at the cadaver.

After the crowds had dissipated from the plaza in order to join the procession, Alma sat at the tree where her father had been slaughtered and began to cry. *Lloro a mares*, they say in Spanish. She wept oceans is what they mean. Alma wept and wept.

She could not cease the weeping. Her tears eventually followed the corpse of her father, which was paraded through the streets with a small marching band playing celebratory music. The crowds were as festive as they were during the yearly processions in honor of Cajabamba's patron saint, la Virgen del Rosario, during the month of October. This time, though, they were not paying homage to a virgin. They were rendering tribute to the depredations of the Shining Path. The stream of *llanto* followed Alma's father, as his body was pulled in front of the church, as it was exhibited in front of the soccer stadium, as it was dragged through the small park where Cajabamba's only swimming pool was located.

Eventually, Juan Carlos Ramos, the eldest son of Cuchillazo and head of the *senderistas*, noticed the stream of tears and was perplexed. Where did this water come from? So, he abandoned the crowds that were celebrating the mayor's death and followed the thin brook formed by Alma's weeping. He followed it through cobblestone streets, through unpaved roads, and through gravel alleys, until he finally reached the plaza, where Alma was still crying. Immediately, he was taken by Alma's beauty—the auburn hair reaching to her shoulders, the green eyes like emeralds, and her youthful figure.

He was used to taking any woman he desired. Such was one of the perks of being the son of Cuchillazo. So, as soon as Juan Carlos saw Alma, he decided that she would be naked in his arms, that he would make her his lover.

"Why are you crying so much?" Cuchillazo's son asked, when he approached her. He was a handsome man, fully Amerindian, with copper skin and jet black hair held back in a ponytail. He was dressed like a *senderista*, with a red kerchief about his neck, green military fatigues, and the red poncho so common in the region.

"I am the mayor's daughter," Alma responded. "I have just witnessed my father's death, and my pain knows no bounds. I cannot stop weeping. Just last week, he was healthy, cheerful, and ruddy-cheeked. Now, he is a naked carcass. What has happened to him is something I never imagined, not in the worst of my nightmares."

"That is revolutionary justice," Cuchillazo's son replied.

"The white man has exploited the Quechua peoples for so long that extreme measures are necessary. We intend to create a new Tahuantinsuyo, but it shall be a Maoist Tahuantinsuyo, ruled by the people's revolutionary vanguard."

"Many of the people of Cajabamba don't even speak Quechua," Alma answered, "and my father was not a white man. He was a *mestizo*, like so many others, a *mestizo* who belonged to the political left. Why must you achieve your ends through violence?"

"Sometimes, bloodshed is necessary to nourish the revolution," responded the son of Cuchillazo, as if he were repeating a *mantra.*

"That's nonsense," Alma replied. "Brutal nonsense in my view." She didn't care if she was speaking to a *senderista.* The events of the morning had left her too fatigued to worry about her own safety.

"Why discuss politics?" Cuchillazo's son queried. "I'll protect you from any further punishment. You just have to be compliant, receptive, shall we say, to my entreaties. Why don't you join me for drinks on Wednesday at the tavern owned by Doña Chana? Then, we'll see what happens."

"Thanks, but I'm awfully busy," Alma replied.

Cuchillazo's son grinned and gazed at her with eyes of irrepressible lust. "You don't have much of a choice, *querida.* I hope you're a smart girl and understand what I mean."

"I'm betrothed to a man by the name of Jesus Aureliano Garcia," Alma said. "I've sworn myself to him, and I will not know another."

"Your lover will never know. We can keep this between us. I suppose you're an intelligent woman, that you know what's best for you."

"I'm a virgin," Alma responded. "My betrothed will know, if I have been with another."

"Do you realize who I am? That my father is now the sole authority in this town? That I am the son of Cuchillazo? Surely, you don't want my father investigating you any further. Women who are found to be reactionary are severely punished. I hope you understand what I mean."

"Yes," Alma shuddered. "I know what that means. For the love of God, please just leave me alone."

"Often, they are gang-raped," Cuchillazo's son continued, his dark, wide eyes piercing her like hot coals, his thin lips twisted into a vague smile. "Sometimes, they are subject to genital mutilation, tortured in all kinds of ways. But with me everything shall be—what's the word?—*bonito*. I promise you that I will be gentle, when I take you in my arms."

"I have sworn my love to Jesus Aureliano Garcia. There is nothing you can do to persuade me."

"We'll see what you think in a couple of days," Cuchillazo's son answered. "I can't see you tonight or tomorrow, because I have some business to attend to with my father, but I'll find out where you live. You can expect me on Wednesday night, at eight o'clock on the dot. Please wear perfume. I love a woman who is fragrant."

The next day, early in the morning, Alma made her way to the house of Mama Josefina, a *curandera* who lived on the outskirts of town. She lived in a small house built of stone, next to a small yard, where she kept a few farm animals and raised corn and potatoes.

Mama Josefina recognized her. She expressed surprise at Alma's visit.

"Alma Vereau," said Mama Josefina. She was wearing the wool skirt and felt hat typical of Amerindian women in the highlands. She looked younger than her years. "What brings you here? God knows you've never sought my help before. You've always entrusted yourself to the white doctor in town, thinking nothing of my gifts or powers."

"I need your help," Alma answered. "I need it desperately."

"Do you need to entice a lover?" Mama Josefina asked. "That always brings young women to me. Or do you need some of my herbs to end a pregnancy? Nobody will find out about it. Or are you the victim of someone's *maleficio*, of some enemy's *mal de ojo*? I am an expert in countering evil forces."

"I am here for none of those reasons," Alma replied. "I need your help to prevent a rape. The son of the *senderista* leader in town has made it clear that he intends to force himself upon me. Do you think you can help me?"

"That is an uncommon request, although I'm sure it won't be in the coming days, now that the *senderistas* are here. Women are caught in the middle of this war between the Shining Path and the military authorities, and both sides rape the native women with impunity. Perhaps, I can assist you with your problem, but I offer no guarantees."

"Whatever you can do, Mama Josefina, whatever it costs. I'll be eternally indebted to you."

"Come inside," said Mama Josefina. "I'm glad you decided to ask for my care, that you realized I am someone who can help you.

The first thing I want you to do is to drink a potion made from the *huachuma* and *misha* plants. That will put you into a trance, so that you can be more open to supernatural powers, so that you will communicate more easily in the spiritual flight."

"I'll do whatever you instruct me, Mama Josefina. Just help me, please. I beg you."

Upon entering the house, Mama Josefina led Alma to her *mesa*, a piece of white cloth spread out on the floor. At this ritual altar, she effected her cures and interventions. To the right stood icons of good, and to the left, icons of evil. Mama Josefina needed to invoke the icons of good to help Alma preserve her chastity. These icons included a crucifix, a ceramic statue of the Inca goddess Pachamama, an image of Saint Cyprian the magician, glass bottles filled with magical flowers, artifacts from ancient Inca ruins, white sugar, and a sword standing upright (a vehicle to call the spirits). Mama Josefina did not use the icons of evil—a gun, a knife, a human skull, or the fanged stone head of a monster from an Inca temple—to cast spells on enemies, as a *bruja* would do. She knew of the evil arts only so that she could manifest her power over the evil afflicting those who sought her aid.

Alma drank the mixture of *huachuma* and *misha* and entered into a trance. Only then did Mama Josefina begin her prayer to the heavenly powers that could help Alma thwart the dark desires of Cuchillazo's son.

"I want you to try to get in touch with various virgin-martyrs," said Mama Josefina, deep in her trance. "Not only the virgin-martyrs of the Catholic faith but also the virgins of our Quechua peoples. Pray with me to Santa Ines, Santa Barbada, Santa Agata, all of whom were tortured or killed for refusing a man's sexual advances; but also pray to Pachamama, world earth, world princess, world virgin, most powerful of Quechua goddesses, and to the Inca virgins of the Sun. They lived their entire lives cloistered like nuns, forbidden from ever seeing a male, often sacrificed like doves or calves to appease their heavenly spouse. Now that they are in Heaven, they are powerful intercessors. Pray to them for deliverance from your enemy."

In a trance, Alma prayed fervently for several hours. Under the spell caused by the potion made from the *huachuma* and *misha* plants, she felt she could speak directly to the virgins in heaven, and so she asked them for relief. At some point, she thought she heard a response, although she wasn't sure if this was real or just the effect of the drugs she had taken.

"I am Santa Barbada," the voice said, "killed for resisting a lover, and I shall guide you in this journey, on your trail of tears." Then, Alma thought she actually saw Tanta Carhua, an Inca virgin of the Sun, in all her regal splendor, a collar of golden peanuts about her neck, a golden scepter in her hand, speaking similar words. Once the effect of Mama Josefina's brew had dissipated, Mama Josefina offered Alma one final warning.

"I have done all that I can do," she told Alma, "but even if the spirits can preserve your chastity, they may not be able to keep you from being punished. After all, the virgin-martyrs all preserved their virginity, but they paid a very heavy price. Most of them ransomed their virginity with their lives."

"I understand that," Alma said, "but I place all my trust in your powers."

"You may need to think twice about whether or not you give yourself to Cuchillazo's son," Mama Josefina continued. "His father is a ruthless man. There's a reason why his nickname is 'Lalo the Knife Wound.' After all, if you give yourself to his son, everything would be over in a few hours. You can come back to me, and I can give you some herbs, so you will not get pregnant."

"I am pledged to Jesus Aureliano Garcia," Alma insisted. "He is the one man I love, and I will not give myself to another, no matter what may happen."

The following Wednesday, at eight o'clock on the dot, Cuchillazo's son appeared at the door of Alma's house, with three of his henchmen. All of them wore red ponchos over olive-green trousers and military-style jackboots, which reached to their knees. All of them stood over six feet tall with dark, deep-set eyes that seemed to betray some hidden cruelty.

Cuchillazo's son and his thugs were all armed, and Alma felt her situation was desperate. Apparently, her prayers to the virgin-martyrs, to Pachamama, and to the virgins of the Sun had all been fruitless.

"Bonita," cried Cuchillazo's son, smelling of liquor. "My Alma, my soul. No need to worry about my companions. We can take it nice and easy and have a good time. Look, I have brought you a bottle of wine."

"I have already told you that I belong to another. You're a handsome man, young and desirable. I'm sure you won't have any difficulty finding a woman willing to share her bed with you."

"I'm not interested in another *ñusta.* I dream only of you, my Alma, my soul."

"A gentleman never takes a woman by force. I'm sure you understand that," Alma said.

"I shall be a gentleman if you let me, and if you don't, I shall be a *cojudo.* It's really up to you, *querida.* I don't want to get my companions involved in all of this."

"Vayanse al carajo," Alma exclaimed. *Go fuck yourselves* is what she meant, though she knew there was nothing she could do to resist them.

Cuchillazo's son said nothing. Two of his men took Alma forcefully by the arms and threw her onto the bed in her room. They locked the door behind them, leaving her alone with her tormentor.

Cuchillazo's son wasted no time. He tore off Alma's blouse. He was prepared to bask in her nakedness, when he saw something startling. Her breasts had shriveled like those of an old woman, and on her face there had grown a monstrous beard.

"What are you, a sorceress?" he cried out. "How is it that you have become a *barbada*?"

"I prayed to Pachamama, defender of virgins, and to Santa Barbada, the bearded female saint who protects women from rape. I told you that I belong to Jesus Aureliano Garcia. The Catholic saints and Inca spirits have rescued me. Now, please leave me alone."

"You're off the hook for now," said Cuchillazo's son. "I cannot kiss that beard nor taste your shrunken chest. I should shoot you now to punish you for this treachery, but I'm sure my father will have other ideas. If you won't let me touch you because you're a virgin, then we shall make sure that you're no longer a virgin. I was trying to be gentle, you stubborn gilt, showing you only kindness. Now, I shall show you horror."

Alma spent a sleepless night, wondering what the words of Cuchillazo's son portended. At dawn, she was still awake, praying unceasingly to the Catholic virgin-martyrs, to Pachamama, also known as the Virgin of Candelaria, and to the Inca virgins of the Sun. She had heard what had happened to women in other towns, women found to be *perras revisionistas* by the Shining Path, traitorous bitches who were paraded naked through the streets, raped by multiple men, their bodies tortured and their eyes gouged out. When she heard the men forcing open the door to her home around nine o'clock in the morning, she trembled and made the sign of the cross. Then, she collapsed, exhausted by fear.

The delegation that appeared in her living room was led by none other than Cuchillazo himself. Cuchillazo was a short, stout man with a scar that ran from neck to forehead, hence the sobriquet the Knife Wound. He had been an anthropology professor at the university at Ayacucho, the same institution where Shining Path founder Abimael Guzman had taught philosophy.

Cuchillazo had been a *senderista* since the beginning of the movement. He was reputed to be ruthless. A popular legend about his scar spoke to his ferocity. Apparently, even after having been slashed through the face with a *chaveta* by a soldier in the Peruvian army, Cuchillazo had continued to fight and had managed to kill his adversary. There was also the rumor that he had once entered an Andean village, where he knew someone had collaborated with the government forces. Unable to identify the guilty party, he had decimated the entire village—women, old men, and children included.

Cuchillazo did not mince words, when he entered Alma's house. "You are a collaborationist cunt. We have discovered that your lover, Jesus Aureliano Garcia, is a sergeant in the Peruvian army and that your whole family is in league with those hostile to the people's revolutionary project. So, you shall be paraded nude through the streets of Cajabamba to Doña Chunga's brothel on Cesar Vallejo Avenue, where you shall spend a week. There, your virginity will become the faintest of memories."

"Of course," his son added, "you still have the opportunity to avoid this punishment, if you behave nicely. I see that you are no longer bearded. It's up to you. We can resolve this now, between the bedsheets."

"I'm pledged to Jesus Aureliano Garcia," Alma responded dryly. "I've already told you that. I won't sleep with any other man willingly, so do whatever you want. Neither you nor your father shall move me with your threats."

"Alright," Cuchillazo ordered his men. "Undress her, and handcuff her. Then, take her on a mule to Doña Chunga's. We'll see what's left of her modesty after the first day in a whorehouse."

As soon as the *senderistas* set Alma upon the mule, however, something miraculous happened. Her auburn hair began to grow profusely. It covered her shoulders. It covered her breasts. It covered her backside and her pubic area. It grew long enough to cover her entire body.

As she was hauled on the mule by one of Cuchillazo's *matones*, the crowds that had assembled on both sides of the street to watch the spectacle began to feel pity for her. It was one thing to have given in to the giddiness of stoning the town's mayor. It was quite another to see a seventeen-year-old girl punished, to see her *pudor*, to see her sense of shame, to see her somehow desecrated because she had refused the advances of Cuchillazo's son. So, one boy tossed a rose at her, as the mule ambled along, and then everyone else started to imitate him. Damn the *senderistas*. There was strength in numbers.

The witnesses to her suffering tossed roses, lilies, lilacs, and flowers of wild verbena, as she passed before them. Roses began falling from the sky, as they had on the day of the death of Saint Rose of Lima. One Amerindian woman, who wore a multilayered, high-waisted skirt and the circular red hat so often used by Quechua women, ran to her and wrapped a white poncho about her shoulders. If Cuchillazo's exercise in cruelty was meant to humiliate Alma in front of the masses, it had the opposite effect. The masses were beginning to side with Alma. They wished her well, and yet everyone knew that she was headed to Doña Chunga's *burdel*, that there was nothing anyone could do to prevent it, to save her from Doña Chunga's omnivorous clients.

The bordello was located on the periphery of the town, a two-story green structure with twelve rooms and a bar on the first floor, where the johns could size up the available women and choose the one they preferred. The walls of the brothel were painted in garish colors, deep purple and bright yellow, and there was an image of Saint Nicolas, patron saint of prostitutes, affixed to one of the walls. Even at mid-day, the whole place was darkened, as if it were evening. The windows were covered with thick purple drapes, and there were only a few dim light bulbs on the ceilings.

The whores were Amerindians, except for one called *la trujillana*. She had blonde hair and blue eyes, so she charged twice as much as the others. When Alma arrived at the cathouse, Doña Chunga looked her up and down, as if evaluating a commodity.

"You'll fetch quite a rate—Mayor Vereau's own daughter, seventeen years old and a virgin, and a white woman, too. Put on some clothes. When the men come, I shall auction you off. The one who takes your virginity will pay a special price. You are certainly the most exquisite of *putas*."

As she said this, Doña Chunga grinned, imagining the money she would make. She was olive-skinned with dark eyes that hovered over purplish circles. Her lips were purple, as well. This sixty-year-old woman no longer worked as a prostitute but continued to dress like one, with a tight skirt and fishnet stockings, and even a black bustier too small for her breasts. Alma thought that she looked like a libidinous *bruja* and shuddered at the idea of being under her dominion. She had the sense that Doña Chunga lusted after her, too.

Within an hour, a huge crowd of at least seventy men had gathered outside the *burdel.* They had all heard about the new prostitute, the mayor's teenage daughter, and they were eager to delight in her flesh.

Doña Chunga immediately made clear that the first one, the one who took Alma's virginity, would pay a special price, at least five hundred *intis.* Then, only three men were willing. Of those three men, Don Genaro Huaman, an Amerindian who was the *varayoc* of a nearby village, bid the highest price.

The money changed hands, and Doña Chunga carefully counted the bills. Only then was he ushered into the cathouse.

Doña Chunga announced to the rest of the men that they would each have to pay three-hundred *intis* to have sex with Alma, and the men protested. A simple *polvo* cost a tenth of that amount. Still, they remained standing in line. Such was the allure of Cajabamba's newest whore.

"Alma," Doña Chunga hollered. "It's time to become a woman. Come and meet the first of your many lovers. You shall have a great many lovers today. I can assure you of that. We'll rake in a bundle, my girl."

As soon as Don Genaro shut the door behind him, he unzipped his pants. He unsheathed his enormous *verga,* more blue than brown and looked at the seventeen-year-old sitting on the bed, as if he meant to devour her.

"Take off your clothes," he ordered. "My plum, my sweet, my rose."

Alma cowered. "Leave me alone," she cried out. "I don't want you to touch me. Don't you know that I am betrothed to Jesus Aureliano Garcia?"

"This is how it is, the first time," Don Genaro said mirthfully. "A virgin is like a wild horse that must be tamed. Come, I'll show you how to *cachar*. I'm a master. You'll soon see."

He slapped Alma. Once, twice, three times.

Alma looked back at him, her eyes despairing. She took in his huge paunch, his ravenous eyes, his massive hands. Surely, she could do nothing to prevent him from raping her.

"Santa Barbada," she cried out. "Let me die like you did to resist an unwelcome lover. Pachamama, *pacha ñusta*, *pacha virgen*, please rescue me."

"You might as well comply," said Don Genaro. He jumped her on the bed and began to grope the space between her legs, searching for her vagina. Alma felt his cold, clammy hands on her flesh and tightened her thighs like a vise.

"No, leave me alone," she pleaded. "Please let me be." She dug her fingernails into his skin in an attempt to stop him, though she knew it would be useless.

And then it happened.

"What's going on?" Don Genaro asked. "What does this darkness mean?"

Just as he had begun to tear off her clothes, to gaze at her naked body, Don Genaro had suddenly been struck blind.

"Don't you know that I am protected by supernatural powers?" Alma said. "By the virgin-martyrs and the chosen virgins of the Sun, by Saint Cyprian and Pachamama. Now, leave this room. Tell everyone what has happened, and perhaps you will regain your sight."

Don Genaro hastily left the room, and he was soon able to see again. He demanded that Doña Chunga return the money he had paid to her.

"That woman is a *bruja*," he exclaimed. "A terrible witch. As soon as I touched her, I lost my sight."

"Well," Doña Chunga laughed. "If a man of your age cannot seduce a wild virgin, that is no reason for your money to be returned. Perhaps, the next man in line will be more adroit at taming the young girl."

But the next man who entered the room where Alma sat on the bed came out in the same condition, except that it took a bit longer for him to regain his sight. The same thing happened to the third man and the fourth man and the fifth man and the sixth man, all of whom had paid handsomely to deflower the virgin. Finally, the men standing crowded outside the brothel figured out what was happening and began to disperse.

Doña Chunga was infuriated. She threw open the door of the room, where young Alma was sitting. "I don't know what you've been doing, but you must realize what will happen if you continue with such conduct. There are things much worse than living as a prostitute. Do you understand what I'm saying?"

"Yes," Alma replied.

"Once Cuchillazo finds out what you've been up to, he'll be angered to no end and will engage in more extreme measures. I don't know if you've heard what the *senderistas* have done in other villages to women who have resisted, and the Peruvian military are no better. With me, you'll have protection. I can assure you of that, but you must learn how to spread your legs, *mi niñita*."

"You should know," Alma replied, "that I'm consecrated to Jesus Aureliano Garcia. Perhaps, you've met him. When he left, I swore that I would wait for him. I have no intention of failing to keep that oath."

The next morning, Cuchillazo and his son arrived at the brothel in a pickup truck, with five or six Amerindians on the cargo bed, all dressed in multi-colored *ponchos* and *chuyos.* When Alma saw Cuchillazo and his son, she was paralyzed with fear. She had thought that the worst was behind her. Now, here they were again. Cuchillazo and his son handcuffed her and shoved her into the front cab of the pickup truck. Her punishment had only just begun, they said.

"I know what the people are saying," Cuchillazo told her. "That your virginity is being preserved by supernatural powers, by the virgin-martyrs and the Inca virgins of the Sun. Remember, though, that all of the virgin-martyrs were ultimately killed in the end."

"Not so," Alma replied, suddenly mustering courage. "Mama Josefina told me that Saint Agata was spared by the Lord."

"Well, you should know that neither saints nor Inca spirits have ever interfered with my work. I have been forced to interrogate dozens of people to find out whether or not they were revisionists, and not once have I been stopped by Christ or Pachamama, or anybody else. I don't think that when I take you to the prison at San Blas you will be protected, either. We're going to excise your breasts with pincers, wretched woman, and I myself intend to gouge out your eyes. And perhaps, for good measure, we'll mutilate your sex, as well."

Alma shuddered. In the lambent sunlight, Cuchillazo's face looked all the more disfigured, his scar purplish and raw. His eyes, small and round, like those of a guinea pig, stared at her with hatred. She had defied him, and there was nothing worse than defying Cuchillazo.

Then, his son intervened. "Of course," he said, "if you consent to spend the night with me, you might be spared."

"No," Cuchillazo retorted. "It doesn't matter if she fucks your brains out. I couldn't care less about your adolescent crush. It's between her and me, now. She thinks she can disobey me with impunity. All the citizens of Cajabamba are laughing at me. We'll show them what it means to defy the head of the people's army."

The prison at San Blas was an unassuming stucco structure, filled with those suspected of conspiring with Peru's military authorities, and even with some leftists who did not toe the party line. As soon as Cuchillazo guided her into the compound, Alma heard the screams, loud wails like those of pigs about to be slaughtered. Many of those screams belonged to Quechua women, accused of collaborating with the enemy, who were being raped or whipped in punishment.

Cuchillazo led her to an underground vault. His son and the Amerindian men in *chuyos* followed close behind. Cuchillazo left the door open at the top of the stairs, so that others might learn of her punishment and be forewarned.

Suddenly, he brandished his pincers, two pieces of metal with blunt concave jaws like the blades of a scissor.

"Where do you want me to begin?" he asked Alma, grinning.

"Please, have mercy," Alma implored amid her tears. "This is an unjust punishment, brutal and undeserved. Justice should be tempered by mercy, Comrade Ramos. Please, I beg you, leave me alone. I beseech you, I pray to you. Please let me be."

"Now is not the time for mercy," Cuchillazo responded. "You have thrown away that opportunity. Let's see if the virgins of the Sun will help you, now."

"Please," Alma repeated.

"I am the Sun now," Cuchillazo pronounced, "and you are in my orbit. Let's begin with your eyes." He laughed.

In all her life, Alma had never encountered pure, unmitigated evil such as his, and now she was under its control.

She felt a sudden and excruciating pain. Until the very last moment, she did not believe Cuchillazo would engage in such brutal behavior. And then, she knew what it meant to be blind. "Please," she cried out in the darkness. "Please, have mercy. It is so much pain."

"Now, we shall excise your breasts," Cuchillazo announced in a gleeful tone.

Alma could not see what he was doing, but she felt the blade at her chest. For Cuchillazo, it was the ultimate act of masculine prowess, the ultimate act of dominion over a woman. So, he cut off her breasts with relish, and then he proceeded to mutilate her pubic area.

"Now, let's see if Pachamama will save you, or the Virgin Mary herself," exclaimed Cuchillazo. He left Alma bleeding on the floor. "Don't fuck with Cuchillazo, or you shall be fucked yourself."

That night, Alma did not die. Nor did she sleep. The pain was too great, the wound too deep, the shock too intense. She had become the pain itself, and her body, the scene of a terrible lost battle. She felt as if her flesh had been taken in and spat out by the dragon of evil, that beast of cruelty dressed in the military fatigues of a man known by the people of the Andes simply as the Knife Wound.

Surely, the virgin-martyrs have abandoned me, she thought. Surely, the Inca virgins of the Sun have forgotten about me. Surely, Pachamama and Santa Barbada have both been asleep, tonight.

The pain gripped her fiercely, as she thought of her condition, a great *dolor* that was not located in any one part of her body but seemed to be everywhere at once.

She sensed the twilight. The faint luminescence rose from the top of the stairs leading to the vault where Cuchillazo and his men had left her. Soon, a faint glow appeared, and she could dimly see the grayish walls, the dirt floor where all her garments had been strewn, and the blood on her own body. As the minutes passed, she saw things in greater and greater detail, as if a spiderweb were gradually being lifted from eyes, no longer vacant.

Gradually, her pain subsided. Her breasts grew back, beautiful and round, and her sex was no longer bloodied. No, it was intact, emanating the smell of a wild rose in bloom.

She thought of her beloved, how she had saved her flower and the nectar of her breasts for him. Her sacred womanly flesh longed for him. Then, a frightful thought interrupted her reveries. What would she do when Cuchillazo's men returned? Surely, they would want to kill her.

But when the guards entered her cell, they didn't touch her. They had heard rumors of what had happened to the men at the brothel. Now, seeing her safe and unbloodied after the torture she had endured the previous night, they were convinced more than ever that she was guarded by supernatural powers. They did not want to be subject to Alma's *maleficios*, to be subjected to the punishments of the gods or goddesses who so obviously protected her.

Still, they alerted Cuchillazo. "The woman you wanted to harm is not only alive but shows no visible signs of torture. We are not going to harm her, since she is defended by preternatural forces. If you want to remove her from the prison and try to punish her further, you are welcome to do so, but we shall not participate, Comrade Cuchillazo," they said.

Cuchillazo was undaunted. When he arrived at the prison, around three o'clock in the afternoon, he had already made his decision. Alma must be killed. A public stoning was impossible, as the *pueblerinos* of Cajabamba would never consent. Already, Alma was being hailed by the Quechua-speaking peoples as virgin of the Sun.

The rumor, probably reported by one of the prison guards, had spread about town that she had survived a grueling night of torture. Cuchillazo feared that he was becoming the laughingstock of the town, the great guerilla warrior defeated by a seventeen-year-old virgin heroine. So, he gave the orders. A pyre was to be built in the center of the plaza, a structure made of wood especially for Alma's execution. That should show anyone else who contemplated resisting him that no one could toy with Cuchillazo.

Cuchillazo was not rough with Alma that afternoon, though he did not fail to handcuff her. He guided her to his SUV and even made sure she wore her seatbelt.

"Where are you taking me?" Alma asked.

"You shall see," Cuchillazo replied in a serene voice. Then, he added, without changing his tone, "You are to be burnt at the stake."

Alma glanced wildly around for any kind of escape, but handcuffed as she was, she couldn't open the door of the vehicle.

"Why do you hate me?" Alma asked, as if she could reason with him. "So much hatred, just because I won't sleep with your son."

"This is the first thing you have to understand, *muñeca*, that I don't hate you. At this point, it is a military decision. I don't want the townspeople of Cajabamba to form *rondas campesinas*, as have been formed in so many other villages, to oppose the hegemony of the Shining Path."

The SUV arrived at the plaza shortly thereafter. Already, a crowd had gathered to witness the execution, some dressed in Western garb, others in the bright colors of the Amerindian raiment. Many of the women wore *wawas* strapped to their backs in shawls, the way the Andean *ñustas* carry their children.

At the north end of the plaza, just in front of what had once been the municipal building, a funeral pyre awaited Alma. Cuchillazo himself tied her to the wooden structure and then began to read the litany of charges, including not only sedition and revisionism, but also witchcraft. However, he soon learned that the people of the plaza were not going to support him.

"Desalmado," they cried out. Soulless is what they meant.

"How can you burn the seventeen-year-old *aclla*. What has she done to deserve such punishment?"

The crowds became more and more heated, more and more emboldened. "If this is what the people's revolution means, then we reject it," someone cried out.

"Down with Cuchillazo," another screamed.

Cuchillazo felt he was losing the crowd, so he made a desperate gambit.

"All right," he said to Alma. "If you accept my son's hand in marriage, then you shall be spared from being burnt at the stake."

He fully expected that Alma, on the doorstep of death, would accept his offer, particularly since he was not offering a one-night tryst but an honorable marriage.

Alma, steadfast as ever, answered, "No, no," and then again, "no."

Cuchillazo, feeling cornered, began to pour the gasoline at the foot of the pyre. He poured it onto Alma's feet, onto her legs, all over her body. One of his henchmen appeared with a lit torch and prepared to burn the recalcitrant virgin.

The crowds protested. They began to whistle and to shout. Some approached the funeral pyre with the desire to liberate the seventeen-year-old Alma, their *aclla*, their virgin-martyr, their virgin of the Sun.

Then, a single shot rang out. Cuchillazo was struck in the face.

Alma looked down at the dead body on the ground and was astonished. She had thought of Cuchillazo as an evil spirit, a *supay* who would never die.

The other *senderistas* did nothing, lest they be ripped to pieces by the throng.

Jesus Aureliano Garcia, still carrying his pistol, rushed to the feet of his beloved.

That night, Alma shared her bed with her betrothed. That night, she was a virgin, a martyr no more.

Antonio Di Bianco

THE MOON OF BARRANQUILLA

One night I will look for you,
because it will no longer be you.
You'll see me coming from afar,
fast enough to blend in with the moon.
One night, you will stop dreaming of me,
because I will be right here, in front of you.
Then, you will hold my hand,
because it will no longer be you.
You may think it is a dream,
but it will only be the moon.
This moon of Barranquilla
that has cradled me so,
because it is my own moon.
It will reveal the truth of my love,
full of secrets,
and you will believe them,
because you will no longer be you.
I who have loved you,
I who come from nowhere,
I who have given you all of me,
I'll stay there with you, under the moon,
like a warrior who throws the axe.
I will stay under the moon with you,
every time that life brings you back to me.
And it will happen, because I know you.
Only look for that moon,

and I will be with you, my love.
Always yours. Look for
that same Barranquilla moon.

E. Martin Pedersen

MY WALDEN POND

No news, good news, bad news.
I don't want news, sports, weather
on the hour, circling the globe.
I can look out the window.
I can hear the wind blow.
I can hear my own thoughts,
and my thoughts about my feelings,
and my feelings.
Do I sound too self-centered,
too introspective, do I?
This is astronaut training.
Nothing is more rigorous,
because nothing is more important.
"Either life is a daring adventure . . ."

Thoreau was right to come back to town in the end.
I'll go back to town, but I need to get ready first.
I don't know all the grasses and flowers.
I haven't given each cricket a name.
Let me see the newborn foxes.
Let me indulge myself in waiting.
I won't carry this beyond all reason,
but I've hung a mailbox on a tree.
When my draft notice comes,
I want to be ready.

Ch'oŭi
Ian Haight, Translator

EXCERPTS FROM HOMAGE TO GREEN TEA

In Master Tasan's poem to Zen Master A-am, "Asking for Tea," he writes:

In the morning, when flowers begin to open
and snowy-white clouds drift in the sunlit sky;
or when waking from sleep in the evening,
the luminous winter moon splitting a jade stream—
these are auspicious times for tea.

. . .

The teas Snow Blossom and Ripened Cloud
compete in fragrance—
Two Springs and Infusion of Sun
have made Jiangxi and Zhejiang provinces famous.
The red mountain of Jianyang County
is well-known for clear water;
the quality of Moonlight on Mountain Streams
and House of the Clouds
are especially respected.

. . .

A silk tent's shade
has an oddly favorable influence

on tea leaves,
so when heating
with a bamboo stove
in a tea contest,
the water must boil calmly.
When using a hot-burning pine charcoal,
choose pure water.

The tea, judged by its richness:
the road fills
with fresh scents of tea—
people forget to return home.

. . .

Decorating tea cakes
with gold-foil dragons
or phoenix
enhances their appearance,
but one hundred cakes
require 10,000 gold coins.

Who can fully realize
the genuine color and fragrance
of tea? A finger's touch
despoils a tea cake—
its true character,
lost.

Epilogue

The season's first tea from Ch'oŭi
steams scents of green,
the first bird-tongue leaves
harvested before the Season of Rain for Grain.
One need not mention
Moonlight on Mountain Water
or House of the Clouds—
We enjoy the year's full cup and smile
at Startling Thunder.

Ana Vidosavljevic

RICE FIELDS

THE RICE FIELDS OF TABANAN were her favorite. Their greenery was endless. She wished never to leave Tabanan for some other place. This was her home, her solace, and her joy.

Lela was walking slowly, a skinny eight-year-old girl. Her dark curls looked even darker, the dirt covering their fine texture, dusting them with gray. She was tired. She felt secure holding onto her mother's hand, but her mother's hand was slippery with sweat and dirt, so she had to let go this hand. Both she and her mother walked on feet full of blisters. They had been walking for hours. The sun had dried their skin, until it became like a snake's skin, rough and warm.

Lela's mother encouraged her to keep walking. She told her that they had to run away from the "civil war," as if it were some strange evil creature that was chasing them. That terrible monster was after them, and they had to cross the border to find a safe haven in some country that was not Syria.

Syria had been her homeland, though only for her early years. When she was very little, she had played in her garden full of flowers and dressed up her dolls. Sometimes, the neighbors' children joined her.

Now, those days were gone. Lela remembered them through a fogged mind. The memories were vague. Time alone had not faded them but also fear and sorrow. She remembered moving from one town to another, from one house to another, from one shelter to another. This is what most of her life had been made of. Here she was now, running again.

She didn't know where exactly they were going, though her mother often mentioned *across the border*. Was it some special place? Was there some peaceful life that waited for them in that land *across the border*? Perhaps, they were they going to settle down, finally safe and far from the monster of "civil war." She hoped so.

They walked continuously for nearly two days, through rare clearings in the woods, far from the open road. Lela was exhausted. Now, she felt a terrible numbness that would not let her continue. Her mother tried to carry her, but the eight-year-old girl, skinny as she was, felt like a heavy burden for a woman so tired. They took longer and longer rests. There was no other solution.

At night, they found a cave in the forest that stretched along the path they followed. Both fell asleep there, only moments after they rested their heads upon the ground.

Lela woke to a strange rumbling. The ground was shaking, and stones were falling down from the ceiling of the cave. She started and cried out to her mother. The cave was dark. She could see almost nothing. She called again to her mother, but there was no answer. The rumbling sound came again.

Were these the bombs that she often feared? Were they falling down from the planes? She groped about the ground where she lay, the ground where her mother was supposed to be. Her hand reached something soft. This was her mother, but her mother was not moving. Lela shook her, trying to wake her up, but her mother remained stubbornly still. Lela began to fear that her mother was unconscious. Perhaps, she had been hit by a falling rock.

Lela grasped her mother under the armpits and tried to drag her from the cave. The woman was not heavy, but for Lela, exhausted as she was, the body felt like lead.

Lela moved slowly, her face dripping with sweat. When she finally reached the entrance of the cave, the moon lit her mother's face, covered with blood. Her lifeless eyes were wide, and a large wound gaped from her forehead.

The shock left Lela immobile. She stared at her mother's lifeless body, unable to move. She did not know how long she stayed like that. Once the realization of the tragedy hit her, tears rushed down her dirty cheeks. They were unstoppable. She cried, until that awful fatigue possessed her fragile body, and in that state, she fell asleep.

She awakened again to strange sounds. There was some kind of commotion and people all around. Her mother's body was covered with a white sheet. Men in grey uniforms and large, heavy boots stood all around. Some of them held rifles.

A tall woman with curly ginger hair approached Lela and asked if she spoke English. Lela knew only a few English words, so she shook her head. Then, the ginger-haired woman left her alone.

After a while, she returned with another woman. This woman was short and looked like the women in Lela's hometown, though a bit darker, with a small nose. She began speaking to Lela in Lela's own language. She wanted to know how Lela had arrived there, where she was from, and for how long she and her mother had been running. She asked if Lela had cousins.

Lela answered some of the questions. She knew well the name of her hometown, but she and her mother had left it behind a long time ago. She couldn't say for sure when or for how long the two of them had been running from the civil war. Yes, she had cousins back home, but she didn't know if they still resided there or if they too had run from that monster of a civil war.

The woman's name was Samira. She worked for some organization that helped refugees.

Lela didn't know what "refugees" were, but since Samira was helping her, she assumed that she was one of them.

Samira brought her hot food and cold water. Soon, they would move on, she said.

Where? Were they going across the border, as her mother had wished to do?

"Yes," Samira said.

After eating the food Samira had given her, Lela slept again. She dreamed of her mother, saw her running through beautiful green fields. The land resembled the fields around her hometown, though the grass was shorter and a darker green. The people working in these fields wore strange pointed hats. Palm and banana trees stood all around.

Lela did not recognize the place, but in the dream, she followed her mother. She came so close to her that she thought she could stretch out her arm and touch her mother's hand, but just then, in the dream, her mother disappeared.

Lela woke sobbing. Her body shook. Samira rushed to the tent, knelt beside Lela, and hugged her. "I am sorry, my dear child, but I am sure your mother is in a better place now," she said. Samira held the girl for a long time. "We will find you a beautiful home," she said. She smiled.

Lela looked up at the woman and believed her.

They spent two days in the tent on that broad field in the valley. People in uniforms buzzed around, talking to one another, talking on phones with large antennas and writing down things that must have been important. They appeared serious and focused.

Then, Samira and two men with dark hair and stern faces took Lela to some town that looked similar to her hometown. The houses were small and well-built, painted white or yellow, though the streets were filthy and full of stray dogs. The people were similar to those she had known back home. Still, this place was unfamiliar to her. Lela thought that she must now be *across the border.*

Samira and the two men drove her to a beautiful white house surrounded by greenery and tall gates, opened only to those who were friends of the people who lived there. Security guards stood out front. Their rifles were large and their faces, unfriendly. Somehow, they smiled discreetly, when they saw her.

Lela was surprised by how large and empty that house was. The walls were hung with paintings, mostly portraits of serious men in uniforms. In one corner, stood a tall glass case filled with medals and trophies.

This was the residency of the American Ambassador, Samira explained.

Lela didn't know who or what the American Ambassador was, but she hoped he was a good man who would help her find safety. She missed her mother. She didn't know whether she could be happy again, so alone now in the world.

Samira took Lela to a spacious room lined with shelves full of books. She told her to have a look at whatever books she found interesting. A man with a rifle remained in the library with Lela, his unsmiling face and eyes directed at the wall. He was in no mood to talk, or perhaps, he did not speak her language.

Lela roamed the large room and gazed at the books on the shelves. She took down a few of them and shuffled through their pages, until she settled down with one. The book was titled *Asia.* Its pages were filled with colorful pictures of places she had never even imagined. A few familiar scenes resembled her own country, but most of the pictures showed new sites that brought pleasure and excitement.

Lela gazed at them, her eyes wide, amazed that such places existed.

Beneath each picture was printed a short description. Almost at the end of the book, she found pictures of the island in Indonesia called Bali. It was splendid, with live volcanoes, pristine beaches, and lush foliage.

As she continued to leaf through the pages, she discovered familiar scenery. This was a rice field in the land called Tabanan. The broad green field with peasants who wore pointed hats was the field from her dream. It was the field where she had seen her mother walking.

She gazed at the picture for a long time. She was not sure for how long exactly, but when Samira entered the room, Lela didn't hear her.

Samira laid a gentle hand upon her shoulder.

"This is my new home," Lela said, pointing to the image of the field.

Samira seemed confused. After few moments, she asked, "Why do you like that place more than the others? This book is full of beautiful places."

"I dreamed about this place."

"Come with me," Samira said.

She walked Lela down a long hallway to a large chamber where the American Ambassador sat behind an enormous desk. He was tall with gray hair cropped short, so that he had a military look. He smiled kindly and promised to find her a "proper home."

He spoke the truth. Within a week, Lela was moved, again. She was placed in an orphanage with hundreds of Syrian children who had also lost their parents. This was how Samira explained the place, though she didn't explain how those children had lost their parents. Was it an accident in a forest cave, or another strange happening that had separated them?

None of them knew where their parents were.

Only Lela knew that her mother had passed away. She knew what had happened, so she didn't have the hope that these hundreds of other children did, the hope that they would soon be reunited with their parents. Lela only wanted to find the home she dreamed of, the home that her mother had wanted for her.

She lived in the orphanage for more than a year, and she got used to the life there. Every morning, the children would wake up at six and eat a simple breakfast of toast, jam, butter, and boiled eggs.

After breakfast, they would hurry to attend classes. The school was in the same building in which they lived, and therefore, their daily life was relegated to that one large gray structure without greenery.

Sometimes, rare birds rested on the window sills. They came to eat the bread crumbs that the children left for them.

Less frequently, the children were taken on excursions to parks, or to picnic on the river bank, but they were always followed by men in uniforms who carried rifles.

Lela wondered why. She guessed that they were not safe. Perhaps, the civil war was still after them.

After dinner, they would watch a film, usually boring, on a big screen that was set up in the dining room. Those who wished to read could go to their bedrooms, instead. The bedrooms were large and filled with bunk beds, where dozens of children slept.

Each day was more or less the same.

The most exciting day for Lela was Sunday. On Sundays, Samira visited her. She would have visited more often, she said, but her work didn't allowed her that. She promised to find Lela a better home one day, and Lela trusted her.

One Sunday, with the sun at its zenith, Samira showed up. She was more cheerful than usual, smiling from ear to ear. Lela knew that she had brought interesting news.

Samira hugged Lela and sat down beside her. Then, she told Lela about a Dutch family who lived in Bali and wanted to adopt her. They had seen photos of Lela and read the reports from her teachers and caregivers. They would fly over in a few days to meet her. If everything went well, Samira said, Lela would, within few weeks, receive the necessary papers and fly to Bali, to her new home.

TWO YEARS PASSED. Now, the girl on the purple bicycle cruised the streets of Tabanan each day, a broad smile on her face.

Lela didn't believe in miracles, but her mother's goodness must have worked wonders for her. She was thankful to her for that. Her dark curls danced in the wind.

Her foster parents were teachers in the school in Canggu near Tabanan, and they were her own teachers, as well. Often, she thought of how lucky she was. She remembered the dream, her mother's and her own. Often, she thanked the spirit of her mother, who she was certain was still with her.

Philip Jason

THE BANG OF SELF

I.

i.
I remember there being more than this
back when the parchment of this life
still smelled like a carcass

ii.
I remember the lofted galaxies
speaking to me like my body
was a language

iii.
I am sure I could feel the wet ink
flowing through my veins

II.

i.
here comes an ancient clan
of village idiot emotions,
false, desperate sensations
belonging to the ugly earth,
where things grow backwards
into the ground toward burial

ii.
all around the clan, organs
fill and chime, while
streetlamps eat shadows, pumpkins
ripen and explode and die
and colors crash

iii.
I am sure I could feel the words of this body
flowing through the galaxies

III.

i.
there once was a boy
who believed
the sky was full of clowns

he sang and sang
and for now, we
will let him sing

ii.
we continue to let him sing

iii.
and continue to let him sing

iv.

boy of the clowns,
the flame in your heart
is the one that sets the world
on fire with love

v.

I swear I could feel the language body pulsing

vi.

I swear I once knew the carcass smell of innocent life

Ziaul Moid Khan

MONI BABA

SOME YEARS AGO, in the countryside of North India, there lived a working man. What his real name was, hardly anybody knew or bothered about. They called him Moni Baba, the silent saint. He had held a clerical position in the Delhi Development Authority. One day, he suddenly turned to spirituality and abruptly stopped speaking. His family was thunder-struck with this, his bizarre decision, and they tried their level best to bring him back to his senses, but to no use.

So, the family locked him up inside a room, and there he was given a good thrashing, beaten black and blue. He was tethered in his chair for hours without food and water. Still, he was adamant and did not speak. He only indicated through gestures and body language that now his path was solemnly different, for he was no longer interested in the mundane world of noisy people and their chatter. His family had no choice but to give way, and Moni Baba embarked upon a spiritual journey.

His office at ITO in New Delhi pressed him to resign from his post, but he scribbled onto a slip of paper and handed it over to the concerned official. It read, "I regard the office rules, but God wants my presence elsewhere, so I'd be on indefinite leave." The officials put the matter under consideration with the higher authorities, and after a while, they buried it in a cold file.

MONI BABA STOPPED GOING to his office altogether. He put on white attire and made his *kutiya*, a hermitage, facing west at Johripuram, out in the countryside. This place was under a *banyan* tree surrounded by two ponds, en-route to the village. There, he meditated and smoked. Soon, the village youngsters took a keen interest in Moni Baba and kept his place buzzing.

At night, disciples would assemble at his place to discuss the various village affairs. Moni Baba listened to them with an I-know-all smile. In pure spiritual ecstasy, a couple of youngsters sang religious folk songs that Baba would enjoy, swaying his head to and fro in tune with the beating of the *dhol* and tongs, played by Tirdi's son. There was one unspoken rule of this congregation. No political issues would be discussed. Sometimes, the village temple priest would join in with the night's assembly to enrich the spiritual learning.

In his spotless white dress, Moni Baba was extremely punctual. He awakened at four in the morning, showered, and worshiped Lord Shiva for hours. Then, he watered his plants and read the Holy Scriptures. He had a dark complexion, sharp features, and long black tresses that fell across his shoulders. His lean frame and formidable height made him an impressive persona.

That year, the village experienced no thunder showers. The *monsoon* season was almost over, but the weather remained dry. The sun-god was spreading his fury, and peasants were worried about their crops of sugarcane, cauliflower, green-chili, and bottle gourd.

The village youngsters discussed this serious matter with Moni Baba, who gestured them to have a *bhandara*, a public feast. Then, he blew his *shankh*, the conch. This was his time for the evening prayer.

The boys, his disciples, went door to door to spread his message among the masses.

The village elders were taken into confidence. Each family was to contribute something small for the *bhandara*. The charity was willingly given, the date was fixed, and the feast was prepared.

Finally, on the auspicious day, all of the arrangements had been made. For transparency of donations, a villager named Surya announced continually through a loudspeaker the name of each and every donor, as well as the amount donated. The underprivileged and beggars were fed to their hearts' content.

That same night, there was heavy rain. A downpour irrigated the entire countryside. People began to put their faith and trust in Moni Baba. From this night forth, he became extremely popular, a household name in the village and beyond.

Henceforth, Moni Baba made it a point to proactively organize a feast every summer, to bring a good rain both for the village and the adjoining countryside. His faith was unshakeable, and the Almighty favored him. Men, women, and children loved this silent saint, who used a sign language to make his point. His name reached far and wide, and in only seven years, he had a large following, even as he remained silent.

One fine morning, he suddenly exclaimed, "Jai ho." People were taken aback. In a little while, the rumor was rife throughout the entire region, and people traveled to his *kutiya* by the thousands to listen to him. Here, Moni Baba delivered his first sermon under the old *banyan* tree.

Surprisingly, the same year, his office in New Delhi issued the pending seven years' salary to his bank account. A verbal pact was agreed upon, and when Moni Baba gave his word, he kept it for life. So, once in a fortnight, he'd visit his office just to sign his attendance.

He used a portion of the funds he received for the construction of a statue of Lord Shiva and the upkeep of his hut. The rest of the sum, he gave to his family.

FROM THE FIRST DAY that Moni Baba had stopped speaking on to seven years later, when he'd suddenly resumed, I'd had a fleeting desire to have a personal interview with him. His *kutiya* was a stone's throw from my residence, and I could easily walk there in seven minutes flat, but for the problem that I could never take time out from my busy life, from my desk.

I'd passed by the hermit's hut several times and saluted him. "Jai ho," he responded with vigor and enthusiasm. Yet, I thought that I should come to visit him well-prepared, with a diary and a pen.

I know that he knew of my writing interest and held a high opinion of it. This, I came to know through people who visited him, frequently.

Precisely speaking, I wanted to write the full story of his life, and for this project, I needed several sittings with him. In those days, I was working to complete a poetry collection, so I kept postponing these meetings.

In 2015, I got married and settled in a city with Mona, my wife. It was then that I lost my link to the village, entirely. Still, deep down, Moni Baba remained alive in some compartment of my brain.

The wish to have a heart-to-heart chat with him, in order to jot down and expose his tale, the higher cause that had made a holy man out of an ordinary human soul, was always there, active and kicking somewhere in me. I did not and could not forget him. I wanted to know of him.

ON JUNE 20, 2019, I received a routine call from the village. It was Shuja, my elder brother. We exchanged generalities and pleasantries, when suddenly I asked him, "How is Moni Baba?"

"Moni Baba is no more," he said.

"How?" I asked him, shocked.

"Nobody knows. He was found dead in his room. It was mysterious, though no police complaint was registered."

I felt my guts wrenching, my throat dry with want for words at the regret of not having had an interview with this pious soul.

"And to respect the departed soul, there was no *bhandara* this year," Shuja added. "In his memory, a temple is being built near his *kutiya* by Rajeev Swami, Gopal Buchha, and Surya, by his disciples and some other villagers. Strangely, the village has yet had a good pre-monsoon rain."

Craig Evenson

MERE CHOICE

The wrong path looked fine,
so I chose it and found
that it stopped
at a broken mill.

It was an optimistic choice
presuming a measure of life in the cards,

more steps
ending at endless dead-ends,
one of the beauties
and mercies of life:
the potential to annihilate by mere choice
all infinitudes
in favor of all others,
to sit down on the warm ruins
and study the reflective face of the river,
becoming and becoming again
and again.

Ever Jones

THE UNRAVELING

Dawn-drenched bird unpacks
our wounds in a song so blue
every stone is the chorus. Silence
with no address wanders our bodies,
like gods looking for prayers or
prayers looking for gods. We will
never truly know the difference.
The headlines written yesterday
throw dirt on the graves of truth,
as we wake up wake up wake up.
In this blue hour, everyone I love
travels the uncertainty of their dreams.
My spirit brushes the matted hair
across their foreheads, an invisible
whisper, while stars dissolve
the wishes they wished. We are here
in this age of the undoing, eyelashes
on our cheeks, while we spend
entire days trying to believe
we are alive. The robin will mate,
and its perfect blue egg will crack
and need to be fed. Faith
is the story we share, until the
fledglings croon for more.

Ever Jones

CONTINUENDING

prayer requires void,
a dark far too faithless
for our ruin

near everywhere, blue window
code of tv scene-switch,
a story in desperate acts

in the apocalypse movie
how many of us are relieved
when the universe fire
smokes earthly life?

i lose you
here
in the details of us, where

wingtips skid
over snowy rooves

and the past cautiously
works a path through
our bodies

talons unclinch prey,
you say
to nowhere

as time slips
and the bedrock of meaning
returns to the earth

Michele Alborg

NEIGHBORS

SO HERE I AM, mopping up another mess. While I am pouring milk into my Saturday morning coffee, Caleb jostles my arm. The hot drink splatters my hands, the counter, and the floor. Before I reach for the sponge, I peer out the kitchen window and entertain a mini-fantasy of flight—my body weightless, rising above the clouds like a runaway balloon, riding the air currents to another dimension. Yeah, right. I've chosen this life. There's nothing to escape. What would the other dimension have that this one doesn't? Fewer chores? More orgasms? Ha. Dream on.

After I glide the sponge over the spill, I do what I always do and push the impulse away. I grab my phone—the best tool of distraction for the midlife crisis demographic. It pings with a text from Zhang. The upcoming condo sales release has thrown the other members of our team into a last-minute frenzy. He's calling an emergency session at the office, starting in two hours.

My husband is off on yet another business trip. He's extended it an extra day, so he can "unwind" with his colleagues, leaving me alone with Caleb. My two best friends have fled for this long weekend in May, and my sister-in-law isn't answering her phone. With everyone out of reach, who will look after Caleb? Although younger employees often show up with their dogs, it's an unwritten law that you can't bring your kid to work, even on a Saturday.

In a panic, I pace the living room. I am swearing like a character from a Tarantino film. Then, I jump into a crazed tidying session. Visual clutter is the enemy, so I ask Caleb to put away his Lego. As usual, he ignores me and dumps more pieces onto the floor.

Instead of becoming unhinged, I take a furtive dip into the ginger snaps and a restorative skim of Goop.com. An article about vaginas reminds me of our neighbour, John. Lifesaver John. My own personal saviour, John. Lovely, wonderful, stay-at-home-dad, John. John with the cool Insta feed, with pic after pic of his motorcycle restoration projects.

He actually answers his cell, an event as rare as a solar eclipse. I clear my throat and swallow my nervousness. I beg, grovel, and try to bribe him with some of my husband's homemade beer. He laughs his good-natured laugh, airy and trouble-free, and invites me to bring Caleb over.

Exactly thirty-eight minutes later, Caleb and I navigate past the jumble of father-and-son sports equipment (Frisbees, baseball bats, skateboards), and I tap at the front door. The newly renovated Vancouver Special gleams with what must be VOC-free paint and sustainably-sourced cedar. Truth be told, I'm more than a little intimidated by John and his chic producer wife. The one time I set foot inside their house—Atlas' sixth birthday party last year—I meekly admired the modern Danish furniture and the spread of organic treats, so gorgeous it could have been photographed for *Kinfolk* magazine.

John comes to the door, and I thrust the litre bottle of stout at him. "Thanks so much for looking after Caleb on short notice. Fred's flying back from Ontario this afternoon, and I have a work emergency. I hope we haven't messed up your Saturday plans." I don't know him well enough to risk a hug, and a handshake seems too formal, so instead, I press my hands together in the sign of prayer. "Namaste, kind sir."

John grins, his eyes crinkling behind his oversized plastic spectacles. The lank white cords dangling from either side of his hoodie accentuate his slender build. A thought flashes through my mind. What does he look like naked? I glance down at his toothpick legs encased in skinny jeans. At school pickup, I've caught other mums eyeing him, a sexy dad who must know his way around a snack and cuddle.

"It's all good, Amanda," he says. "Julie's away at a premiere, so it'll just be Caleb, Atlas, and me. If the weather holds, we'll hit the park."

"I apologize in advance, if Caleb eats you out of house and home."

"I'll feed him fruit loops and pop." John pauses, like a child after a knock-knock joke, then grins too widely. "Kidding!"

Like a runner-up pageant queen, I keep a smile glued to my face. Is he sizing me up, too? I'm older than he is and must look like a haggard crone in my mum jeans and sweatshirt. I should have put on some concealer and a swipe of lip-gloss. Too late now. Like ten years too late. "Sometimes, Caleb's not great at listening and forgets to use his words. He likes to range, so please keep an eye on him."

John leans against the doorjamb with one hand on his hip. Is that a streak of purple in his salt-and-pepper hair? "We'll be fine."

Caleb darts into the foyer. "I love your house, Atlas' Dad." He speaks in his newly acquired otherworldly voice—Where did he pick up that affectation? Without waiting for an answer, he tears through the house and opens a door onto what I hope is a fenced backyard. Atlas races after him.

Time to get the hell out of here. "You can call my cell, if you need to." I shuffle backwards and pause, one foot lingering along the top step. "We'll have you over for gin and tonics this summer. Thanks again."

John's lip curls with the faintest hint of sarcasm. "It's my pleasure."

I don't have the time to fret over John's tone. After a few more hasty words of thanks, I dash to my car and weave toward the downtown pinnacles of concrete and glass. The sidewalks are crowded with young couples who are enjoying the sunshine. Easy smiles, hands lying idle on asses, lips brushing cheeks. I'm forced to bear witness to this spectacle from the prison of my vehicle.

Once upon a time, during the first months with Fred, we spent our nights sharing childhood insecurities and exploring our kinks, back when I prided myself on experimentation and spontaneity and didn't mind the slather of his semen. Back then, our life had been expansive, infinite. Now, the days are clamped tight, over-structured and over-scheduled. No way out, no breathing space or room for error.

The traffic is entangled at Hastings and Main. I roll down my window to get some air. A starling alights from a tree, its spotted belly quivering in the warm morning sunshine. As it lopes upward, it shits, and the goo lands on my hood with a plop.

I turn on the radio, but the song is too peppy and high-pitched. I fondle my phone. My ex-boyfriend, Drake, lives on this block. Texting him would be a very bad idea. How could I put the yearning, disappointment, and misplaced lust into words?

How U doing? Eggplant emoji. Like a lunatic, I press send. Within nanoseconds, I regret the text and burn with humiliation. Why aren't there more nuanced emojis and a warning to stop you from behaving like a moron?

Emojis aren't the problem, I realize. I'm the problem.

It's not like I want to go to Drake's stinky apartment, with the piles of empty whiskey bottles in the recycling bin and dog hair, everywhere. Besides, why would he bother with me after ten years? Most likely, he's bonking some young, pert specimen at this very moment. Or recovering from said bonk, lying on his futon and drinking instant espresso, with absolutely nothing to do and no responsibilities, whatsoever.

My phone lights up with a response from him. Hey Mads. What U up2?

I write back. Sorry, that was meant for someone else.

He replies with a dismissive smiley face.

Okay. I vow I will no longer, under any circumstance, continue to behave like an idiot.

Twenty minutes later, I march into the office. Already damp, I roll up my sweatshirt sleeves. There is no AC on the weekends. Zhang nods hello, as he scribbles sales targets onto the whiteboard. No one comments on my tardiness. Soon enough, however, Barney quips about development costs, and Dana storms out, apparently insulted and inconsolable. After a short search, I locate her, as she stares out the window at a wheeling seagull, cursing under her breath. We return to the conference room and pick up where we'd left off. If only we could agree on a division of assignments, we'd be on our merry ways. Another argument flares up, this time about the website. We are nowhere near a consensus.

Slightly high from the marker fumes, I check out Zhang. He's wearing shorts, and his arms are unbelievably smooth. I could lube him up, and we'd ooze all over each other, like seals on a slip-n-slide. The image is so disgusting that I can't help but feel aroused. He turns toward me, just as I lick my lips.

"Whoa, Amanda, your neck is all red. Can I get you a glass of water?"

"It's okay. I'm fine. You're fine. Everyone's fine."

"Maybe, you should go for a walk outside? It's pretty hot in here."

"No, let's get this over with." I laugh. "Bet you've never heard that before. I mean, we're almost done." I shuffle a pile of papers, and with an odd sense of foreboding, I glance at the digital clock. Two hours have passed, since I arrived. Time is slipping away. My life is slipping away. My sanity, gone.

Finally, we finish with a tentative plan for Tuesday. I'm the last to leave. I pause for a moment before pressing the down button for the elevator, then delight in the Pavlovian ping, as the steel doors slide open.

A text buzzes from my purse. It's John. Hey, Amanda, could you give me a call?

Uh-oh. What's Caleb done now? Has John connected the dots back to my lacklustre mothering? I press the call button on my phone, mentally rehearsing an apology.

John answers, his voice tight and clipped. "Amanda? Don't worry because it just happened, but . . ." He stops and gives a quick, sharp exhale.

"Yes?" I utter with too much edge. I haven't eaten today, other than the ginger snaps. My blood sugar is low, and my patience is not what it could be.

"Caleb was playing with Atlas . . ." His voice trails off again.

"Is something wrong?"

"He's, well . . . I've gone up and down the street and talked to everyone who's around, but I'm not sure where he is."

The elevator doors open again, and I step out into the parkade. "Wait—what?"

"Honestly, it was the strangest thing. The boys were playing in the backyard, while I was making lunch. I called them in, but Caleb didn't come. I checked everywhere, inside and out. Couldn't find him."

"I don't understand. Did he leave your yard?"

"I lock the rear gate during playdates. He may have climbed over the fence or up the maple tree, onto our neighbour's garage. He couldn't have gone far. Don't worry. We'll find him." He enunciates each word carefully, as if he's worried.

I might go full Carrie on him. I might. My heart starts to pound, and sweat dampens my forehead. Behind my eyelids, there's a burst of violence. Knives slice, limbs scatter. This is due punishment for John's carelessness, for letting my son wander off. Rivulets of blood ooze, ruining his pristine furniture. I wipe away the perspiration. Where did I park? "He probably went home. He knows where the spare key is hidden," I say.

"I already went to your house, and there's no sign of him. Mum's coming to look after Atlas. You and I can search the neighbourhood. I'm sure we'll find him."

"Search?" I echo. "Okay, I'll be right there." With a beep of the fob, I find my car and stumble into the driver's seat. I am behind the wheel, now. The seat belt offers the fleeting comfort of restraint, before I zoom out into the treacherous world. Ahead, some damn Mercedes stops. Why does anyone care about traffic lights?

Fred. Is he still in the air? I can't do the math on his flight time. I take a wrong turn. A homeless man is gathering items he dropped at the intersection. I swerve, narrowly missing him—He's somebody's son, somebody's lost boy. Where is his mother? I press the accelerator, the tires sliding backwards. What if Caleb has been abducted? What if someone is hurting him? I feel a stab of nausea. Two more blocks. The road ribbons, a long curve right, and right again. I won't make it in time.

I pull up to the curb in front of my house. John jogs over and opens my car door, an impertinence that annoys me. I glare at him.

"Amanda," John's voice is treble, like a spoon tapped on crystal. The sound brings me back to my rational self, or a facsimile of one.

"Don't worry. We'll comb every inch of Grandview Woodland, before nightfall," he says.

I try to answer, my gaze locked on the sweep of his bangs, but no words come. An older woman who shares John's thin lips approaches with Atlas in tow. Atlas looks the way I feel—terrified.

I get out of the car, brush past John, and kneel on the damp grass in front of Atlas. "What happened when you last saw Caleb? What exactly were you doing?"

The boy leans into the folds of his grandmother's dress. "He changed."

"Changed?" I repeat, trying to keep my voice even.

"He got all feathery."

I stare at him in disbelief. "Did he climb over the fence?"

"We were making a magic potion from leaves and water, and then he got kind of mean."

"Did he say something?"

"Yeah, he said, 'Watch this.' Then, he jumped really high. He grew wings and flew into the sky." Atlas shoves his thumb into his mouth and his grandmother gently tugs it out.

I begin to shake. Something, just one thing, better start making sense, before my brain shuts down, permanently. "I need to go look for him," I say.

John puts his hand on my arm. "I'll go with you."

"I'll stay here," John's mum says. "And I'll pray for Caleb."

Pray? I don't trust myself to respond. I shake off John's hand, pivot, and head toward home.

Within moments, I'm on my front porch. Caleb's bike is prone beside me. It's quiet, and there aren't any lights on inside. I can't go in. Not now. Caleb's shoes will be by the door, his half-eaten breakfast on the table, his Legos on the carpet. I have to calm down. But what if I can't find him? What if Caleb has disappeared into the clouds, never to return? No, it's simply not possible.

From a thousand miles away, I ask John, "Did you guys go to the park?"

"No, we didn't go anywhere."

I race down the front path and back onto the sidewalk. My pace is swift, decisive. "Caleb," I yell, as I weave from the sidewalk to the road and back again. "Caleb."

John trails behind me. He is dark and flat as a shadow.

Ahead, a dogwood stands in full, creamy bloom. As we approach, a crow swoops from the branches, sailing directly toward me, its blank, beady eye trained on me, its wing grazing my hair. I duck, and it circles, dips, and drops down for another attack. I yelp and cover my head with my arms. It flutters back to the sky in a grand arc, swerves and dive-bombs again. I'm ready for it this time, and I swat the creature hard with my purse, hard enough to send it crashing to the grass. It lies there for a moment, opening and closing its black beak. Sickened, I approach. I've hurt the crow unnecessarily, maimed a bird that had been instinctively protecting a nest. I bend down to scoop it up, but it hops on brittle legs, before launching up and over the roof.

I stand for a moment, trying to catch my breath. John comes to my side. "That was nuts. The bird, I mean." With his hand visibly trembling, he pulls out a vaping pen and takes a puff.

Something inside me shifts. He's clearly incapable of minding children. Look at him, with his ironic band t-shirt, checkered Vans, and vaping pen. How could I have been so stupid as to trust him with my son?

I stare straight ahead, unblinking, my voice slimy as a log in a forest stream. "Were you smoking weed, when you lost Caleb?"

"What? This is nicotine. I told you. I was making lunch. It happened so fast, like something from a dream. One minute he was there, and the next minute he was gone."

"You're not telling the truth. Tell me what happened. I deserve to know."

"What the hell, Amanda? I know you're really stressed right now, but you need to stay calm—"

"Were you watching porn?"

He tugs off his glasses and presses his hands to his eyes. "For Christ's sake, Amanda—"

"Oh, I get it. You were screwing someone in the bedroom, while your wife's away? Have I got that right, John?"

"You've gone completely crazy. Look, Caleb was outside alone, okay. In the backyard."

Ah, finally. The real story. "Alone? Why?"

"I had the back door open, and I heard Caleb shout, 'Shut the fuck up, you dumb cunt,' to Atlas. I thought it would be best for Caleb to, you know, have a time out."

I stop walking, trying to understand what he's saying. I can't imagine my son using the 'c' word. "Wait, what did he say?"

"Who knows where kids pick these things up? It wasn't a big deal. I brought Atlas inside to set the table. A few minutes later, when I called Caleb in for lunch, that's when I realized he'd disappeared. I said it before, and I'll say it again. I'm sorry. We'll find him. I know we will."

The park at the end of our block is eerily empty for such a warm spring evening. The sky glows toward the west, illuminating the swings and monkey bars, the covered slide, the washroom building. I check everywhere. Nothing. I approach the enormous cedar tree at the edge of the park, the one the older children love to climb. The upper branches sway in the breeze. I tilt my head back, scanning the dark mass.

Above, Caleb's silhouette perches on an upper branch, at least forty feet up.

"Caleb," I scream.

"Mum?" comes the feeble reply.

John takes a few steps toward the tree. In profile, his jaw and high cheekbones remind me of Drake. "Hey, buddy. What are you doing up there? You gotta come down. Your mother's scared to death."

Caleb's voice flutters down. "I like it up here."

"Please come down," I yell. "It's past your bedtime, sweetie."

"I can't. It's too far."

"Stay there," John says, sloughing off his hoodie. "I'll come get you." He grabs the lowest bough and clambers up, huffing and grunting, his sneakers skidding over the rough bark. He climbs to the next bough, and the next, pausing every fifteen feet or so to look down at me. I can only see Caleb's silhouette in the fading light. I turn on my phone's flashlight, but it barely illuminates the space in front of me. Branches rub and jostle, and I hear John and Caleb talking. I can't make out what they're saying. I wait, watching a line of ants march along the trunk, blue spots in the LED light.

Then, John's foot appears in the circle of light, and he drops to the ground, with Caleb clinging to his back.

Caleb flies into my arms. "Mum."

"What were you doing up there, sweetie? I was so worried."

"Can I go back up tomorrow? I could see downtown to your work. All the way to the ocean and mountains. I watched the streetlights come on and a bunch of airplanes. It was so cool. I wish I could stay there forever." He yawns and buries his face in my shoulder. His small body goes limp against mine.

"I'm so glad you're safe. Let's get you home." I should demand answers or at least scold him for using the 'c' word, but I don't. As we walk toward home, memories overlay one another. The fruity-sweet scent of Caleb's hair after a bath. The infinite span between coughs during a winter cold. The sound of us singing Neil Young songs off-key, before bed. I could have lost so much, everything, but now he's back. It's going to be okay.

Although he's much too heavy, I carry him, holding him close, his hands gripping the back of my sweatshirt. The three of us trudge up the front steps. Once inside, in the living room, everything's quiet and peaceful.

I lay Caleb down on the couch and drape a blanket over him. "Are you thirsty, baby?"

He looks as though he's struggling to keep his eyes open. "Yeah," he says.

"How about a glass of milk?"

He nods, almost asleep. I leave John and Caleb, and I dash to the kitchen. Hands shaking, I yank open the fridge door. The milk bottle falls out and crashes to the floor. I step back, burying my face in my hands. "I don't know why I did that," I say into my hands. "I think I've lost my mind."

John bends down to pick up the shards of glass, carefully layering them in his palm.

I shake my head. "I didn't mean to take this out on you, John. I'm so nuts lately. Caleb's always running off. I guess a part of me is jealous of his spirit. I'm not making sense."

"It's cool—" he dumps the glass into the bin and pauses, as if gauging my volatility, "and if you need some edibles to help you unwind, you know where to find me."

I snap my head around and glare at him.

"Kidding. Sorry. I shouldn't joke about weed. My bad. What a day, eh? He must have been up in that tree for hours. Crazy. Anyway, I hope we can laugh about it, someday. Now, if you're okay, I think I'll head home." He edges toward the door.

Behind John, the doorknob turns, and with a squeal of hinges, Fred enters. He is cradling a crow in one hand and pulling his luggage with the other. He parks his bag by the front closet and shifts the bird into a cradle-like embrace.

"Oh. Hi, John." Fred's gaze roves from me to John, and then finally rests on Caleb, who is now sleeping with noisy, hiccupy snores on the couch. "Sorry I'm late. It took forever to de-ice the wings. Anyway, I found this little guy on the front lawn. He's hurt. Do we have a shoebox we could put him in?"

The bird lets out a loud squawk and flaps its wing frantically. It trains its black eye on me, shiny and round with terror.

Fred grips the bird tightly to his chest and folds the wing against the creature's belly. It closes its eyes and its beak opens, silent and limp.

No one moves.

It must be the bird that attacked me earlier. Fitting. "I guess it finally died," I say, biting my lip and stifling a giggle.

"Don't say that." Fred looks at me with wide, tired eyes. "It's not dead yet." He runs his index and middle fingers along the length of the bird's body, caressing the feathers with tenderness. "I can still feel its little heart beating."

I giggle again, and despite my husband's quizzical expression and John's clear discomfort, I laugh some more. I laugh because Fred and Caleb and John are funny, their certainty and their conviction, my fury and my forgiveness—all so damn funny.

"I stand corrected," I say. And I mean it.

Stuart Silverman

STOPPING. LOOKING. SEEING

"pretty high for a moth," I say to myself,
a dingy yellow sun afloat in a pallor of haze

neighbors pile on dead leaves,
the air's blindsided by smoke

now, the moth moves, or I see it moving,
an airborne dance, the twist in a hurry

when I look again, only a golden flutter,
dips and swirls of a *danseur*, then still, it seems

swooning into arms held out, falling against
the codpiece swollen with sunlight

the tutu it wears, its own self, the sway
captive to its whim inventing being

the moth, no longer flittering along gutters,
runs rings around the house,

tunnels leaf-packed and soggy,
a chamber of dead flies and mold

the moth, drunk with spring, does a dipsy-doodle
a little woozy, I think I hear taxis in full honk-and-swerve

avoiding, but only just, a loitering couple,
an old man jabbing his cane, a sewer rat *in extremis*

now the moth floats along the side of the house,
parallels the chestnut trim edging an outside wall

now, it is resting, a blotch of dull yellow caught by the sky
and, now, a curlicue circling the garden

and tired of the dance, or sated, it
hovers over the grass in a paroxysm of indecision

until a primrose woos it with open petals,
hunger stoking desire

and the moth makes a beeline for the stamen,
scenting the moist air with its ripe appeal

Mosque | Michael T. Smith

Stuart Silverman

IMPRESSION, EAST RIVER

The water leaps the wooden piers.
    A drift of clouds is pushing by.
The surface darkens, but it clears,
    constant, to an inconstant sky.

The water leaps the wooden piers.
    A gull emits its raucous cry,
which, counterfeiting anguish veers
    across the slow, quiescent eye.

The water leaps the wooden piers.
    The sun throws down a midday high.
A scrap of brassy light uprears;
    indifferently, the clouds reply.

The water leaps the wooden piers,
    desperate as a clutch of fry.
Complicit with the changing spheres,
    the early ferry drafts a sigh.

The water leaps the wooden piers,
    whose time-soaked boards as one deny
the droplets raining down in spears
    to give the river god the lie.

The water leaps the wooden piers.
  An angler gives it one more try.
Around the bend, some muted cheers,
  no one to posit where, or why.

Richard Leise

BEE

What Mallory had on display sold, more than anything because it was a wondrous novelty that also yielded to well-worn ideals. While the mechanical Bee was great, much greater was consumer desire. And so for any customer, while Mallory presented a lazy or laconic sort of unprofessionalism—one which, from just about any other customer service representative elicited responses ranging from anger and scorn to rage and derision, emotions that often swelled to inform a sort of righteous indignation—here, at this particular kiosk, in the presence of this particular girl, these sentiments, when experienced, were ultimately passing. The girl was special, not slow.

Today's consumer—a woman with her young son—was so filled with desire that she did not feel in any way disrespected or put out by what, according to any other metric concerning sales, was an affront, an offensive display, at least somewhat uniquely personal. When wrestling with desire, Americans, at least those like the woman, come to accept, if not outright expect, certain degrees of disaffection. This was how the world worked.

More than anything, however, this woman wasn't paying attention. Mallory, as far as the woman was concerned, was about as real as the mechanical Bee.

The mother—her son was not yet seven—pointed up toward the Bee and flapped her hands like a bird. Mallory shrugged with a series of slow, seemingly unrelated movements, nodded, and produced, from a locked cabinet near her feet, a small wooden box.

The box itself appeared so plain and so ugly that anything by way of artwork carved upon its lid and sides mirrored Michelangelo. For all but the aesthete, this was the case.

On the sides of the box were carved images of a honeybee, which was drawing pollen from carefully crafted flowers—salvia, wisteria, poppy, honeysuckle. The flowers functioned to illustrate childhood innocence. At least, it was possible to think this way.

On the top of the box, a young girl with open hand reached out for, or possibly released, a bee. The young girl wore a long-sleeved dress, pinafore, bonnet, and ankle boots. She was at once anachronistic and timeless, difficult to ascribe to any one era. It was this, our current climate of irony and mistrust, which offered unto her likeness such naked relief. As if carved from fallen light, the girl, smooth and rounded, was beautiful. When considered from different angles, the girl shone, bespeckled amid muted burgundies and cosmic golds, oceanic grays, and cyanic blues. She appeared, like a field of wilting wildflowers, to reflect rather than absorb a recent rainfall. She reminded one of something once desiccated, now growing fuller.

The caricature made more of an impression than the colors themselves did, and the light accenting the girls' shoulders gleamed with the astral patina of a summer afternoon, the slow gloaming oncoming. Hands cupped, arms outstretched, she rose like a sprite, the toes of only one foot on the ground.

Mallory opened the box for the woman and her young son. Inside the box was a Bee. Scaled to size, the toy, for all its startling accuracy, was strangely disturbing. Gone (even if you had been stung or were terrified of flying insects) was any sense of fright. The sensation was confusing, like taking a sip from a can and discovering that what tastes red is, in reality, green.

Mallory, who opened the box at the kiosk every afternoon, five days a week, seemed unimpressed. Her expression functioned to heighten the consumer's level of interest, which had, in this short time, segued to become something beyond curiosity and closer to voyeurism, as if she were spying or had been let in on a secret.

Mallory's generation still held beauty as a spiritual ideal. That which nature has forever proposed through her mysterious acts of creation, Mallory's contemporaries sought to mechanize. People worked to mass-produce holiness through an erasure of mysticism, in favor of what one could not term a broad secularization but, rather, a society steeped in a queer brew of isolation; one which celebrated a new species of the heightened, self-indulgent human; the screen of whose device, like a sort of lidless eye, offered, if you performed even a cursory search, a window unto the soul.

The mother broke through Mallory's reverie with a question. Confused, Mallory just nodded her head.

To a girl whose interests are isolate, detached from the mass production of the decade, Mallory possessed an accompanying morality, which made her soul ache with understanding. Absent of incongruity, devoid of disdain for anything other than what served an immediate purpose (or satisfied a definite need), Mallory lived her life with the grace of a young woman afforded the strength of spirit, wherein her passion existed so as, to quote a phrase, "to find an antidote for the emptiness of existence." In short, she wanted to be happy, and Mallory sought happiness absent of concern or self-consciousness.

Mallory blithely lived through the present moment of her own created history. Those who didn't know her considered her happy. And who is to say?

Having no real interest in beauty, let alone the force to go about assessing or creating it, Mallory remained open, possessing nothing but the belief in all that she believed. Mallory experienced neither pride nor shame, however remotely, in her world's collected wisdom about beauty and truth.

And so, because the Bee seemed so real, Mallory instinctively knew that it wasn't. The Bee had to have been manufactured. Real bees didn't look so genuine. Buzzing, flitting from flower to flower, bees moved much too quickly for meaningful observation. The bees Mallory had observed closely were dead, littering sidewalks and grass parks like cigarette butts. Every bee she had seen had been unique, somehow weird, but this facsimile was too accurate.

Mallory believed—though she had no words for this—that being inanimate wasn't necessarily permanent. So, she wished life for the Bee.

She understood that states were impermanent, and she believed that everything, even something dead or man-made, could somehow be wrought, like magic, into the lovely discord and broken harmony of the living, of consciousness, that place where objects lose through time their vitality—this shared space where, in essence, we are created not only, but specifically, to die. So, while living, most of us spend far too much time either worrying about dying, or the things we have done.

But Mallory was just twenty-one. She sparkled. In bloom, her soul shimmered.

Someone much older, who understands the fragile tone of life, might marvel at the grace of her consciousness, this spiritual creature who, in accordance with nature, ascribed to no law, kneeled to no theory, existed upon—or as—that plane, where harmony and understanding recede into a spectral cosmic expansion.

None of this was to suggest that the Bee contradicted any aspect of Mallory's nature. It was just that, at first sight, and this without yet knowing what the Bee could produce, Mallory, in her limited way, was unable to process the product's significance.

How like a beautifully rendered drawing was this Bee, as if it were comprised of imaginary colors, as if the artist had expertly worked outside the lines. A cool sort of halo wavered around the tiny toy, so that the Bee appeared to be internally lit, and so naturally falling light was seen to rest just above its plastic exoskeleton.

There was no doubt about it. The Bee cast a luminous radiance.

THE MOTHER REPEATED her question.

Mallory smiled.

The woman nodded.

Mallory nodded.

The woman smiled.

Nothing.

And so the woman looked down upon her child, and she affected happiness. Ease.

Mallory thumbed through her phone, opened an application, closed another, and set the phone to the side.

The woman looked from Mallory to her phone, to the Bee, and back to her child.

Mallory shrugged and then nodded, again. She reached for her phone and pushed a button. The Bee fluttered its wings, creating a distinct, rhythmic buzzing. This was audible, even over the surrounding din—for the kiosk was located near the Food Court. The toy crawled up and out of its box, and then the Bee was off. Surprised—she had been having problems with the device all day—Mallory clapped and smiled.

The mechanism rose high into the air, buzzing first around the head of the child, whose mother's smile wavered, and then zipping and zagging into and out of any number of nearby shops. Once again, the Bee flew close to the kiosk, before rising and, like a balloon, rising higher still within a remote region of the mall, before becoming all but lost in the convex of a rain-stained skylight. But still, as if this were a function of its nature, the Bee made certain it was visible, was seen, and this miraculously—by creating a psychedelic sunbeam sort of shimmer, the vibration of its wings pooling the air, so as to collect a potent calliope of color.

And then, the Bee fell.

A thread of color poured from the Bee, like Hawaiian Punch, and the Bee, as if struck dead, dropped. The mother gasped, but as if preordained, the toy rose upon an air current to dip and, with a refined air, finally alight upon a table, where it rested unnoticed, silent, and motionless.

People aren't prepared to be amazed, so those in the mall either walked by, or if sitting, blindly gazed upon what they next planned to put into their mouths, neglecting the Bee's generous splendor, the puddled lavender and green light its buzzing wings swept about, the toy's jellybean-like carapace from which yellow spikes, like downy tufts, provided contrast against prison-bar stripes. Oh, but if they had.

How their souls, in spirit, would have risen, flushed with color.

In no way, despite its finite totality, is the Bee an accurate reflection of nature's idyllic splendor. How could it be, when the toy was nearly swatted four times? How could it be, when in so many rational adults, the Bee instilled a heady, irrational aversion? The toy slowly crawled across a table and inspected a tipped cup, the puddle from a pineapple smoothie congealing in a smooth mass, glittering with dimension. A woman, barely stifling a scream, grabbed her tray and staggered from her seat. A man, dressed in a suit, carrying his laptop and a Styrofoam cup of coffee, immediately readied himself to take her place. Then, noticing the toy, he surveyed the Food Court, as if examining those willing to sit within range of the pest. His face was a mask of pure disgust. People didn't understand that the Bee wasn't a bee.

The mother frowned.

Mallory smiled. Flights were always funny.

Still now, as if considering the spill, the Bee regained all of its color, and its inner gleam pulsed, a gradual brightening and dimming that created a discernible shadow. The color grew so intense that, within the jagged beauty of childhood perception, some thought or idea was amplified.

A little boy at the kiosk became possessed of a certainty, an expression manifest upon his face like a strange sort of prudence.

Do words give rise to thought?

Who's to say. If they don't, though, what would we think? If there are no words for this, a picture would be the only way to articulate the little boy's face.

Another woman—another mother—dragged her child by his upper arm. Balanced in her left hand was a tray of food. They stepped together without rhythm. They were a couple, absent of rhyme, their two faces, a unified sort of countenance.

The blunt force of her impatience transformed into something like euphoria, when the woman discovered the open table. Who cared about a little mess? What was there in an empty cup?

But her child would not sit down. The kid wouldn't budge. The mother set their tray onto the table. She freed the bags threaded up near her elbow and dropped them to the ground. She didn't understand. She didn't want to know what was bothering the little boy. Then, her face transformed with a new expression, now almost pretty. The woman appeared happy. She was excited to smash the Bee with the heel of a Teva.

She missed.

She spilled her soda.

The Bee lifted off from the surface and hovered, circumvolved, darted this way and that, wavered, the toy full of incessant movement, the Bee seemingly at once undecided and full of purpose. It circled the woman as if it might attack, and the woman turned. She swung her sandal with surprising athleticism, though how difficult it is to swat a real bee, let alone an object programmed to survive.

Mallory laughed when the Bee rose, made a line for the kiosk, and flew straight up as if blasted by a geyser, before landing, as designed, back in its box.

The boy made some kind of a demand.

His mother whirled, as if bitten, though he had only asked a question. Then, she smiled, crouched, and answered, "Well, it's real in that it's an object, a thing, here in this mall, right there in the box before us. But no, sweetie. No, it's not a bumble bee. It's a facsimile, you see?"

She smiled. She pointed, as Mallory adjusted something on the side of the toy's box.

And then, lips straining, smiling into her child's blank, pointless face, she said, "Facsimile. That means a copy. That means it's not the real thing, real as in being an actual bug, a bee. It's just a toy. A very nice toy, but just a toy. You knew that already, though, right? You understand what I mean?"

She was pleased with her diction. She had spent a year working on her verbal communication, and here were the dividends. The woman smiled and looked around, as if expecting a round of applause.

The boy poked at the box. He said, "Yeah, but is it alive? I want to know if it will actually eat honey."

Mallory began to speak. She pushed through her memories regarding the manufacturer's limited life-time warranty. Five minutes later, Mallory was still talking, and the little boy was crying.

His mother waved her hand. She took her wallet from her purse and told Mallory to stop.

The boy was crying, but his mother was smiling. She led him from the kiosk and handed the child his Bee.

MALLORY HELD THE BEE in one hand. With her other hand, she grabbed the phone. She said, "Call Marcia," nodded and then shook her head, waiting, listening to her phone ring.

And then, "Oh man, thank you. Can you talk?"

"Yeah."

"Listen, have you ever seen, on the Bee, the counter-thingy."

"The owhatamer?"

"Right, yeah. That thing. Whatever it's called. You ever seen it?"

"Right. Yeah. I've never noticed that thing."

"I don't even know if it really exists."

"I don't know. Why?"

"Because," Mallory said. Crying, she lowered the phone and looked up toward the ceiling. She was so tired of misunderstanding, of nothing coming easily. She wiped her eyes with the back of her hand.

And then, "Because I was hoping you'd know. I've never sold one before, and I think I gave them the one, you know," Mallory said, picking up the original box. "I think I just sold the main one. The protégé or whatever. If I don't fly one at least twenty times a—" she broke off.

"Wait, what?"

"Yeah," she laughed. She sniffled. "I actually sold one. But because I've never sold one—"

"Oh, who even knows?"

"It was part of the training, wasn't it? I think? But I can't even turn this other one on. At least, I think it's a different one. They all look so—" She rubbed the bottom of the Bee.

"Huh?"

"Are you even listening?"

"I guess."

More evidence that this conversation was of a meaningless history. Nothing important enough to document. To record. Far more interesting—not that Mallory would think to ask—would be to have the Bee engage in flights, endlessly. Why not? Why ever let the contraption come to rest?

Simple answer. That which is obvious is ignored. Anything, after you have seen it before, or enough, becomes ordinary.

Grounded, however, the purpose of the Bee was threefold. First, to confirm that the experience of each flight is non-recurring, and so belongs only to the observer. Second, to assert that the Bee has flown and landed safely before, thus assuring a level of reality greater in degree, an implication of providential design dictating that the Bee will, once purchased, fly again (and this upon the owner's command). And finally, to demonstrate that they, the consumers, are meaningful, only insofar as they are seen to relate to the flight of the Bee.

Yes. Certainly. What the philosopher says is true.

Art demands a particular point of view.

ANAH, WHOSE MOTHER WAS SHOPPING for a birthday present, saw the words *Is that a bumble bee?* spinning across the smooth, waxed floor. The object clattered, a sound that grew louder as Anah, forgetting her mother, set off to examine the object, quickly closing the distance between the Bee and herself.

The image of a bee as the Bee was amazing. Anah was surprised to see how the toy was made with such wonderful detail. The toy incited the sort of excitement and curiosity that she experienced during the holidays, or at the creek, flipping rocks. The Bee was remarkable. So remarkable, in fact, that Anah, stooping to snatch at it, thought of nothing else.

The Bee was at once heavier and lighter than Anah had expected. This, coupled with the fact that the Bee was even more lifelike in her hand—was suddenly, Anah believed, real—accounted for her mishandling, for her fumbling with the toy. Frightened that the Bee was going to sting, or, worse, bite her, Anah suddenly dropped the toy.

As the Bee fell, Anah raised her hands to her mouth. The toy hit the ground and, like a skipped stone, skittered across the smooth, waxed floor. The people walking the concourse did not notice; the people did not slow.

Absently kicked by someone, the Bee spun wildly in dozens upon dozens of tight, dizzy circles, before, accidentally activated and pointlessly buzzing, it slowed to a stop.

Not dead, but not alive, either.

Anah's concern expanded to become a balloon of misery. She believed she had broken the thing. Her eyes bright with tears, she forgot to breathe. Her face grew so red that it looked as if she would pop, were it poked. Misery ceded to fear, a powerful terror for which the only possible foundation was confusion.

Surfacing from within this terror, simmering but not quite ready to boil, was a sensation often associated with adolescence; that feeling being, of course, embarrassment. Shame.

Unlike an adolescent, however, Anah immediately sought not escape but comfort. Comfort, for a girl Anah's age, was Mother.

The realization that she could not find Mother crashed upon her consciousness. Her little knees buckled, and she wept. How like floodwater, these tears. Anah moved to breathe, but the world no longer contained oxygen, only an element as thick and salty as the ocean. Her tears made bright prisms of the world around her, so that she did not see but only heard Mallory approaching, softly speaking to her.

THE LITTLE GIRL WAS A GIFT. As she approached the child, Mallory disregarded her own troubles, chiding herself for having given in to them. Mallory didn't care about some dumb Bee that rich parents bought for their kids. It's not like the thing was hers, and she had dropped the Bee four or five times a day, herself. The Bee, through no fault of her own, had even flown into walls, been swatted to the ground, and fallen, its battery dead, from great heights. The Bee had been smashed countless times with a hammer—a jeweler's hammer, kept for demonstration purposes in a drawer under the counter.

Stooping to retrieve the toy, she straightened and placed a hand on the little girl's shoulder. If her job was good for anything, it was that this year of speaking with strangers had made her comfortable speaking with just about anyone.

Life was funny, when you thought things through.

"Hey, there. You okay? There's no need to cry. Thank you for finding my Bee."

Anah was not supposed to talk to strangers. On the other hand, she was supposed to be polite. Her mother seemed to place equal importance on both rules.

And then, there was the Bee, which she had picked up and then dropped. Her understanding, a belief all but beat into her by Mother, whenever she reached to touch something, was that everything inside the mall was expensive.

Dumbstruck, Anah didn't know what to do.

"Here, see?" Mallory offered her the toy. "I sell them, over there. It's fine. You gonna hold it again? You see how it's just fine, perfect?"

Anah nodded, and she tracked in her peripheral vision, her mother's approach. She mistook the skip in her mother's step for something other than anger, her grimace for a smile. Knowing that she hadn't done anything wrong—she hadn't spoken to the stranger—Anah was excited that the Bee was still intact, that the girl was willing to let her hold it again.

She couldn't wait to show the toy to her mother. Perhaps, her mother would buy her one.

Still, determined not to speak to a stranger, Anah only nodded in response to Mallory.

She smiled more broadly when Mallory said, "I know the Bee can seem kinda freaky. It looks so real, like it could sting and everything, but it can't. Plus, it's really cool. Did you see it flying? I can show you how it flies. And can you see now that it's fine?"

Mallory tapped the toy atop Anah's head. "This here Bee can take a beating."

There is nothing quite like the smile that accompanies relief, the welling up of a certain joy. Having for the last few minutes wavered between feelings of bewilderment and doom, Anah now laughed.

And then, just like that, there was Mother.

Just as before, Anah's stomach rose and as quickly fell, her tiny knees wobbling. Gone, wiped completely from her sense of being, was the feeling that anything was the matter. Her face was shiny, flushed with excitement.

Anah couldn't wait to show Mother, not so much the Bee, but that Mallory, the girl from the kiosk, had given her such an expensive toy to hold.

And so, Anah was off balance. Laughing, she was unsteady when she raised the toy, when she offered the Bee to Mother.

WITHOUT REGARD, ANAH'S MOTHER had pushed her way through an opposing crowd. The tension that, like an icicle had formed inside her stomach, now blazed. The warmth of relief spread through her at the sight of her child, but much too quickly. Her emotions dissolved so rapidly that these created another, a memetic sort of energy. Her sense of self frothing, she was not in control.

Her vision blurry from crying, she did not understand that the hand outstretched by her face was her own. She did not see Anah. She thought only of what could have happened, her child lost.

Palm open, wielding all the force of worry, she smacked her child across the face.

Anah fell. She dropped the Bee, which went shooting across the floor, as she braced for the ground. Her elbow smacked the tile with such force that, for the moment, she did not feel her face—her cheek already red, and the formed welt rising—sting.

CONTRIBUTOR NOTES

MICHELE ALBORG is a published short story writer and emerging novelist. Her work has appeared in *Berkeley Fiction Review*, *Blank Spaces Magazine*, the *New Quarterly*, and *Blood and Bourbon*. She lives in Vancouver, Canada.

HILA AMIT is the author of a collection of short stories, *Moving on from Bliss* (Am-Oved, 2016). The collection was awarded the Israeli Ministry of Culture Prize for Debut Authors and was recently selected as one of the best ten books published in Hebrew in the last ten years. Her non-fiction book, *A Queer Way Out—The Politics of Queer Emigration from Israel* (SUNY Press, 2018), was awarded the Book Award of the Middle Eastern Women Studies' Association for 2019. *Family* (Am-Oved, 2021), a novel, was recently published in Hebrew. Her fiction has appeared in *Emrys Journal*, the *Washington Square Review*, and *Lilith & Jalta*. One of her short stories was recently selected for the Sue Lile Inman Fiction Award by the Emrys Foundation.

EDWARD BRUCE BYNUM, Ph.D., A.B.P.P., is a clinical psychologist and the Director of Behavioral Medicine at the University of Massachusetts Health Services in Amherst. A student of Chandrasekharananad Saraswati and a winner of the Abraham H. Maslow award from the American Psychological Association, he is the author of four books, including *Dark Light Consciousness* (Inner Traditions, 2012).

CH'OŬI (1786-1866) was a Korean Buddhist monk given a traditional Confucian education, making him a uniquely trained scholar of his time. Ch'oŭi is considered one of the first pre-eminent experts on the subject of green tea in Korea.

CRAIG CZURY is the author of *Fifteen Stones* (NYQ Books, 2017), a collection of short prose from Italy, Chile, and the spaces between. *Thumb Notes Almanac: Hitchhiking the Marcellus Shale* (FootHills, 2016) is his collection of docu-poems based on observations and interviews noted while hitchhiking around his home, the northeastern Pennsylvania 'fracking' region. Czury lives, teaches, gives lectures & readings, and organizes poetry events in the United States, Italy, Albania, and Lithuania. For more information, please visit www.craigczury.com.

DANIEL DE LEON is a writer and musician from Chicago. His work has been nominated for Best of the Net and appears in, or is forthcoming from, *Maudlin House*, *Queen Mob's Teahouse*, *The Other Stories* podcast, and *Secondhand Stories* podcast, among others. He is a regular contributor to the Chicago live lit soundscape. For further reading, please visit www.deleoncreation.com or follow @deleoncreation on Instagram.

ANTONIO DI BIANCO is an Italian psychologist who speaks four languages and has been writing since the age of sixteen. He has published without stopping since 2011. He writes poems, as well as song lyrics, articles, and short stories. To date, he has published in Venezuela, Italy, Colombia, Mexico, Argentina, Chile, Peru, the United States, Brazil, Republic of San Marino, Romania, and Spain. He writes in Italian, English, Spanish, Portuguese and Romanian.

CRAIG EVENSON is a public school teacher. His poems have appeared in a number of magazines, including *Barrow Street*, *Midwest Quarterly*, and the *Louisville Review*. He lives in Minnesota with some cats, some dogs, some birds, and one woman who, as a general rule, does not like his writing. The others have no opinion.

IAN HAIGHT is the author of *Celadon*, winner of the First Book Prize in poetry from Unicorn Press in 2017. With T'ae-yŏng Hŏ, Ian is the translator of *Red Rain on a Spring Mountain: The Complete Poems of Nansŏrhŏn* (White Pine, 2024) and *Homage to Green Tea* by the Korean monk, Ch'oŭi (White Pine, 2023). For more information, please visit www.ianhaight.com.

PHILIP JASON'S stories can be found in magazines such as *Prairie Schooner*, the *Pinch*, and *Ninth Letter*. His poetry appears in *Spillway*, *Lake Effect*, *Indianapolis Review*, and *Hawaii Pacific Review*. His first poetry collection, *I Don't Understand Why It's Crazy to Hear the Beautiful Songs of Nonexistent Birds*, is forthcoming from Fernwood Press. For more information, please visit www.philipjason.com.

EVER JONES is the author of two poetry collections: *nightsong* (Sundress Publications, 2020) and *Wilderness Lessons* (futurecycle press, 2016). His work has been published by *POETRY*, *Tupelo Quarterly*, *Poetry Northwest*, and many other journals. He has been a Professor of Creative Writing at the University of Tacoma for over ten years.

ZIAUL MOID KHAN is a speculative fiction author, romantic poet, and modern philosopher from Johri in the North India countryside. He considers himself a world citizen. His work has been featured in *Literary Orphans*, *Better Than Starbucks*, *Sequoia Speaks*, *To Live Again: An Anthology* (Antimony and Elder Lace Press, 2020), and other publications. Khan writes in English, is mostly self-taught, and resides in Jaipur, Rajasthan with his wife, Khushboo and son, Brahmaand Cosmos. Email him at ziamoidkhan.b@gmail.com.

HAREENDRAN KALLINKEEL lives in Kerala, India. After a stint of fifteen years in a police organization and five years in the Special Forces, he is now focused on writing. Recent publications include *Pif*, *New Reader*, *As You Were: The Military Review*, *Reality Break Press*, *Palabras*, *Queen Mobs*, and *Pennsylvania Literary Journal*. His works are forthcoming in *Djed Press*, *Bryant Literary Review*, *Corner Bar*, *Literally Stories*, and *Phenomenal Literature*.

RICHARD LEISE writes and teaches outside Ithaca, New York. A fellow from Old Dominion University's M.F.A. program, his fiction and poetry are featured in numerous publications. He is the author of a unique literary work, *Johannes & Merritt* (Dark Lake Publishing, 2022) and a novella, *Being Dead* (Brigids Gate Press, 2023). Follow him on Twitter @coy_harlingen.

ALEXANDER MERCANT is an emerging writer based in Brooklyn, New York. He's a former drug addict, a seeker of the Divine, and is currently working on his debut novella. His Twitter handle is @ alexmercant.

EMILY MURPHY is a poet living and writing in Philadelphia. Her work has appeared or is forthcoming in *Manzano Mountain Review*, *Beech Street Review*, *Inklette*, and *Garbanzo*, and is also carried by a very talented pigeon, who delivers hand-rolled poems to upper story apartments. You can follow her on Twitter @weightsandmeans

E. Martin Pedersen, originally from San Francisco, has lived for over forty years in eastern Sicily, where he taught English at the local university. His poetry has appeared most recently in *Adirondack Review*, *Better Than Starbucks*, *Brief Wilderness*, *Danse Macabre*, and *Thirteen Myna Birds*. Martin is an alumnus of the Community of Writers. He has published two collections of haiku, *Bitter Pills* (Cyberwit.net, 2020) and *Smart Pills* (Cyberwit.net, 2021), as well as a chapbook, *Exile's Choice* (Kelsay Books, 2021). A full collection, *Method & Madness*, is forthcoming from Odyssey Press.

Patrick Pfister's most recent books are *Far From Home* (Spuyten Duyvil Press, 2018) and *North Beach Hotel* (Spuyten Duyvil Press, 2019). He is also the author of a poetry collection, *El Camino and Other Travel Poems* (Literary Laundry, 2013). His poems have appeared in various literary magazines. Currently, he is directing the documentary film, *Poetry, New York*.

Sandro Francisco Piedrahita is an American writer of Ecuadorian and Peruvian descent. He holds a degree in Comparative Literature from Yale University and a law degree from Harvard Law School. Most of his stories have to do with Latin American mythical or historical themes, told with a modern twist. He learned to write about Latin America from his grandmother, who told him fascinating stories about growing up in the highlands of Cajabamba, Peru, a town not dissimilar from Gabriel Garcia Marquez's Macondo.

THOMAS PIEKARSKI is a former editor of the *California State Poetry Quarterly*. His poetry and interviews have appeared in publications internationally, including *Florida English Journal*, *Poetry Salzburg*, *Pennsylvania Literary Journal*, *Boston Poetry Magazine*, and *Mandala Journal*. He has published a travel book, *Aurora California* (2021). His recent poetry books include *Monterey Bay Adventures* (2019) and *Ballad of Billy the Kid* (2018).

PETER L. SCAMARDO has had writing published by the *Houston Chronicle* and the *Key Reporter*.

STUART SILVERMAN is an East Coast expatriate retired from university teaching. He divides his domestic life between Hot Springs, Arkansas and Chicago, Illinois. Some 700 of his poems and translations appear in 100+ journals, here and abroad. His third book of poetry is *Drifters* (Atmosphere Press, 2021). He sees poetry as an art, not primarily a form of self-expression but a way to convey experience to a reader, whether realistic or fantastic, which may expand his or her sense of being.

MICHAEL T. SMITH has published over 150 pieces (poetry and prose) in over 80 different journals. He loves to travel and take photos of his destinations.

JOSEPH THOMAS is a poet working hard to see his work published and shared. His serious pursuit of this goal began upon his release from a one-year sentence in the Los Angeles County Jail, where he realized that his lifelong study of poetry—he has a Ph.D. from U.C.S.B. in literature—was a prologue to what he really wants to do, which is write. He lives in Los Angeles, where he spends his time writing, hiking, and being the best father he can to his three children. As a younger man, he spent half a year traveling through India, backpacking and taking classes in various temples.

ANA VIDOSAVLJEVIC is from Serbia and currently lives in Indonesia. She is a teacher, international relations specialist, writer, translator, interpreter, journalist, surfer, and mom-to-be. Her first collection of short stories is *Mermaids* (Adelaide Books, 2019). Her memoir *Flower Thieves* was published by the same publishing house in April 2020.

KWONG KWOK WAI is a former television journalist who has won numerous awards for news documentaries on Hong Kong political issues. Born in colonial Hong Kong, he witnessed the ups and downs of the now Chinese-ruled city over the past three decades. His works explore the national identity and human dignity problems faced by his fellow citizens. He has published three novels and a short story collection in Chinese.

SARAH WALKO is a director, curator, writer, and artist. She is currently the Director of Education and Community Engagement at the Visual Arts Center of New Jersey. She has directed nonprofit arts organizations and executed independent curatorial projects for the past fifteen years. She recently co-authored a graphic memoir, *With Our Whole Broken Hearts* (Highcomms LLC, 2018), and is working on a second book project. Her visual art exhibitions include *Case Studies* at Gallery Aferro, *So That I Might Speak to You of Your Magnificence* at Hudson Valley College, *Raising the Temperature* at the Queens Museum of Art and *Preternatural* at the Museum of Nature in Canada. Walko is also a published author of fiction and nonfiction essays. She was a recent presenter at the National Organization for Arts and Health conference and the New York City Museum Educators conference.

SAMAN ZOLEIKHAEI is a Kurdish poet and graduate of English literature. He has translated James Joyce's *Exiles* into Kurdish, published in 2018. He is currently working on a translation of Kurdish poems into English. He is the author of more than ten collections of poetry.

SUBSCRIBE

110 West 86th St., Suite 5D
New York, NY 10024

____$14 One-Year Subscribtion (one annual issue)

____$26 Two-Year Subscription (two annual issues)

Please include $4.95 for postage and handling and enclose a check written to *Lalitamba.*

Begin my subscription with issue of year __________

Name ____________________________________

Address __________________________________

City, State, Zip ____________________________

Please send a gift subscription to:

Begin the subscription with issue number ____

Name ____________________________________

Address __________________________________

City, State, Zip ____________________________

CHINTAMANI BOOKS

www.chintamanibooks.org

Chintamani Books is a 501(c)3 non-profit press that was founded to offer book donations to hospital patients, prison inmates, and the homeless population.

We published our first volume at the request of a dedicated group of detox patients at the Addiction Institute, who had experienced our inpatient poetry-and-meditation workshops and wished to study further. Since then, we have grown to offer good reads in fiction, nonfiction, poetry, and translation. Chintamani Books is also the publisher of the *Ganga Review*.

To submit, please send a proposal letter and sample pages/full manuscript in hard copy to:

Ganga Review/Chintamani Books
110 West 86th St., Suite 5D
New York, NY 10024

Please include SASE for reply. If you would like your manuscript returned, please provide postage; otherwise, the manuscript will be recycled.

NOTE: Poetry manuscripts should include at least 65 poems/pages.

www.ingramcontent.com/pod-product-compliance
Lightning Source LLC
Chambersburg PA
CBHW021951230726
48463CB00030B/246
* 9 7 8 1 7 3 2 4 5 4 1 3 2 *